Religion
on the
Healing
Edge

Religion
on the
Healing
Edge

What
Bahá'ís
Believe

by Frank Stetzer

Bahá'í
PUBLISHING
Wilmette, Illinois

Bahá'í Publishing
415 Linden Avenue, Wilmette, Illinois 60091-2844

10   09   08   07   4   3   2   1

Library of Congress Cataloging-in-Publication Data
Stetzer, Frank.
   Religion on the healing edge : what Bahá'is believe / by Frank
Stetzer.
         p. cm.
   Includes bibliographical references and index.
   ISBN-13: 978-1-931847-44-5 (alk. paper)
   ISBN-10: 1-931847-44-4 (alk. paper)
         1. Bahai Faith—Doctrines. I. Title.

BP365.S75 2007
297'.32—dc22

                    2007060816

Cover design by Tracy Heckel of Guten Tag! www.gutentag.us
Book design by Suni D. Hannan

Contents

A Note to the Reader

Persian and Arabic words have been transliterated following the pattern set by Shoghi Effendi, the Guardian of the Bahá'í Faith. Also, as a sign of respect, pronouns associated with the Manifestations of God have been capitalized.

Foreword

Early in my investigation of the Bahá'í religion, I returned to the four Gospels, the root of my Christian faith, with the question, "If I were reading these stories for the first time, how would I know that Jesus is who He claims to be, the Christ?" It soon became clear that, for me, the proof of Jesus's divinity is not in His miracles, or even in His birth and resurrection. It is in His deeds and especially His words. These words contain a love, wisdom, authority, and most of all, a truth that is not of this world: "Because he taught them as one who had authority."[1] Instinctively I know these are the words of God, not of man, as certainly as the sheep must know the voice of the shepherd.

When I read the words of Bahá'u'lláh, the divine teacher of the Bahá'í religion, I find this same heavenly power, authority, love, wisdom, and truth. This short book is an exploration of the Bahá'í beliefs and teachings that I, personally, find so illuminating, surprising, ennobling, uplifting, stunning, and sometimes upsetting, challenging, and just plain contrary to the conventional ways of thinking and doing, that I know they must be from God.

The ability to speak eloquently is held in high regard in the teachings of the Bahá'í religion. From an early age, Bahá'í children are instructed and encouraged to stand before an audience and give polished presentations, recite prayers, and give musical and artistic performances. Perhaps I became a Bahá'í too late in my life, but eloquent speech has always eluded me. The more passionate I am about a topic, the less

I am able to express myself clearly. Of all the topics on which I am tempted to open my mouth, I am the most passionate about the Bahá'í religion. So I have put on paper the words I always wished I could say. If nothing else, I can read this short book to people.

I would like to acknowledge a few of the many people who have taught me something that has contributed to this book. First, two faculty members from my undergraduate days at the University of Wisconsin-LaCrosse, where I was to first learn of the Bahá'í religion: Ms. Brenda Randolph, who presented her beliefs with grace and dignity to a mostly hostile audience of which I was fortunate to be a member; and Mr. Wig DeMoville, who helped me to see the "big picture" of the Bahá'í religion. Second, my philosophy instructor at UW-L, Mr. Ron Glass, who tried to teach me to think and write clearly. And finally, my wife Rosemary and our children Darwin, Russell, and Emily Joy, who every day teach me what it means to be a Bahá'í.

Introduction

Ask the average "man on the street" what Bahá'ís believe and
what Bahá'ís do. If you get any answer at all, it will probably
be that Bahá'ís believe God loves all people and that all religions are good, and that Bahá'ís are nice people who try to
get along with everyone. They might be described as innocu-
ous, harmless, boring at parties, maybe even naive or utopian, but the term "cutting edge" will probably not be used
to describe either Bahá'ís or their beliefs.

Do not be misled by the mild-as-milk demeanor. While
many Bahá'ís might seem to be the antithesis of confrontational, they are on a cutting edge of their own design—really more of a *healing* edge—with an audacious plan to
change the ways people, institutions, and nations behave and
interact. The changes they envisage are so fundamental that
they effectively amount to replacing nations and their institutions with new nations and new institutions, and the world's
inhabitants with a new race of people.

There are many religions in the world; some with billions
of followers, others with only a handful. All began with a
central mission, a vision of how the world can and must be
made better; all held that certain beliefs, behaviors, practices,
and institutions were necessary to realize this vision. The
purpose of this book is to demonstrate that, out of all the
possible missions to which a religion could be committed,
the Bahá'í vision, which is to establish a new global civilization founded on the recognition of the oneness and wholeness
of humankind, is the most bold, audacious, original, and

probably the most difficult to achieve, and that the Bahá'í beliefs, practices, and institutions are the most challenging and exciting to be part of.

This book examines the beliefs animating the Bahá'í religion and the practices by which they intend to change the world. It begins with a brief exploration of Bahá'í history and theology. The first four chapters identify four fundamental *defining beliefs* about God, humanity, religion, and history. Bahá'ís are people who, having accepted these beliefs, find themselves inspired and empowered to change their lives by adopting certain specific new ways of doing, or *distinctive practices,* which are described in the next eleven chapters. (The distinction of beliefs from practices is somewhat arbitrary and primarily a pedagogical tool on my part; it solves the problem of where to start. I hope the reader finds it useful.) By embracing these beliefs and concentrating their actions through these practices, Bahá'ís are confident they can actually become a fundamentally different people than any who have ever inhabited the planet. They can build completely new institutions and ultimately guide the nations to a new era in human history.

There are excellent books that investigate the history and teachings of the Bahá'í Faith in much more depth and detail than is attempted here. Much of its history and many of its teachings are comfortably similar to those of the other great world religions. The emphasis of this book is primarily on those dimensions that are new and distinctive, which challenge us to understand religion, civilization, and spirituality in a new way, to become something far better than we are and to commit ourselves to building something more vast than most people, even the Bahá'ís themselves, can comprehend. This is religion on the healing edge.

As will be clear by the end of chapter 1, the Bahá'í religion is scripture-based. Its sacred texts are the foundation of its teachings. On these are built a body of understandings and interpretations that are shared by all Bahá'ís. Last and definitely least are the personal and private understandings every individual Bahá'í reaches during his encounter with the teachings. All three are included in this book. Use of first-person pronouns, such as "I believe that . . ." or "My understanding is . . . ," indicate where my own interpretations and inspirations begin. If they are not completely on topic, they are quarantined to footnotes.

The choice of particular topics is also mine alone. Other Bahá'ís would choose to organize their book very differently. For another perspective, find other Bahá'ís and ask them about the teachings of their religion that they could not live without.

A Note on Spirituality

This book uses the word *spiritual* on almost every page—the spiritual world (or plane), spiritual people, practices, capacities, and institutions. Many people feel comfortable with this word and will glide right over it without a second thought, others will find it confusing and a few will feel it a call to battle, in one way or another. This is not a book about theology, nor am I qualified to write one, but since the Bahá'í Faith is centrally concerned with the spiritual, it is necessary to give at least a working definition. It is not my intention to try to convince you that the Bahá'í understanding of spiritual is better than some other, but just to convey how Bahá'ís use the word and what it means to them.

A person is said to be "spiritual" when he believes that the material, tangible world is not all there is. Behind it, somehow hidden from our five senses, there lies another, more fundamental reality. What's more, he believes that these two realities are interconnected and even intertwined, and that people live in both worlds simultaneously. What different communities believe about this reality varies; religious people in the Western tradition (including Bahá'ís) believe in a creating, loving, guiding God, His Holy Messengers and their teachings and scriptures; they believe in the Holy Spirit and a Covenant that connects God to people, and an eternal human soul created by Him that lives within each person. Other traditions may believe in many gods, the life forces of nature, the spirits of ancestors, eternal virtues and values such as truth, beauty, love, and justice, or simply the ideas of right and wrong. To be spiritual is to believe in this unseen reality and its relevance for daily life.

To act in a spiritual way is to conform your actions to the truth of this reality, as you understand it. Since a person exists in both worlds, actions in the material have ramifications in the spiritual, and conversely, spiritual forces have material effects. For example, the religious person prays, asking God for guidance, healing, or courage. He believes that God hears his prayer and that, in His wisdom, God may answer the prayer and he materially benefits. This act of prayer is spiritual because the supplicant believes God hears and answers prayer; to pray without the belief is not spiritual. Spiritual practices are just spiritual acts that are performed regularly by all members of a community; for example, the practice of daily prayer, the observance of a period of fasting, or of coming together for worship and study. A spiritual institution is a practice that is accepted as having some formal, ongoing status in both worlds, and may involve many members of the community. Examples might be a religious marriage, a pilgrimage, a funeral, or a formal worship service.

Wars probably have been fought over minor differences in what people understand by the word *spiritual*. Although the Bahá'í writings are a rich mine of new insights into the realities of the spiritual world, including the power of prayer, the nature of the afterlife, and the meaning of evil, to split hairs over these realities is not the task of this book, nor is it in keeping with the spirit of Bahá'u'lláh's teachings as I understand them. But it is important to point out that the real opposite of spirituality is to believe man exists in the material world alone, and that God or other spiritual entities, if they exist at all, are not connected or involved in the human world.

Popular culture is full of alternative paths to spirituality. If you are someone who does not believe in God or in the existence of a spiritual reality, but wants to investigate its possibility, you have many options. The Bahá'í writings offer one reasonable path. It is, as described in chapter 2, to first free yourself from preconceived doctrines, ideas, and attachments, then to study the holy books with an open mind, ask God to guide you, and be patient.

1

The Bahá'í Covenant

To explain the first defining belief of the Bahá'ís, it is necessary to start with a short overview of the history of their religion. This will introduce the central figures of the Bahá'í religion, identify some fundamental Bahá'í institutions, and give context to the material that follows. Understanding this first defining belief, the Bahá'í Covenant, is central to understanding the Bahá'í Faith. Several of the threads started here will be developed in subsequent chapters.

The Inception of the Bahá'í Religion

The 1840s were a time of millennial expectation both in Christianity and Islam. In particular, a straightforward interpretation of prophecies in the Old Testament book of Daniel pointed to the year 1844 (1260 AH in the Islamic calendar) as "the time of the end," when God's mysteries would be revealed and the world as it was known would cease to exist. Many Christians anticipated the return of Christ, the Day of Judgment, and the resurrection of the dead.[1] Similarly, Islamic prophecies led many Shia Muslims to expect the appearance of a great redeemer, the *Qá'im*, or "He who shall arise," to be followed by the return of the Twelfth Imam,* while Sunni Muslims anticipated the appear-

---

* Shia Islam predicts a thousand-year interval during which God's guidance is withheld from the world (see the Koran, 32:5). For Shia Muslims, this interval began with the disappearance of the Twelfth Imam in AD 844.

ance of another messianic figure, the *Mahdí*. Various scriptural scholars had different expectations of exactly what would transpire, with many predicting great convulsions in the physical world, perhaps even the destruction of the planet itself.

In 1844, an Islamic scholar named Siyyid Kázim was certain the time had come for the appearance of the Qá'im, and he instructed his pupils to scatter across Persia (now Iran) and Iraq in search of Him. Guided by prayer and their teacher's instructions, seventeen of them would arrive in the southern Persian city of Shiraz over the course of a few months. There, each one separately found the object of their common quest, a young merchant named Siyyid 'Alí-Muḥammad, Who announced that He was the one foretold in the ancient prophecies. Although He claimed to be a divine Messenger equal in station to Abraham, Moses, Jesus, and Muḥammad (the Messengers recognized by Islam) and produced a large body of written scripture in Persian and Arabic, He made it clear that the duration of His religion was to be very brief. The fundamental purpose of His teaching was to prepare a body of dedicated believers for another, much greater teacher, "Him Whom God shall make manifest," Who was to follow in a few years. He adopted the title *the Báb,* Arabic for "the Gate," which symbolized His mission of preparing the way for the appearance of another.

The Báb's teachings spread very rapidly across Persia, and His followers, called *Bábís,* soon numbered in the hundreds of thousands, to the alarm of members of the conservative Islamic clergy and their colleagues in the government. Persecutions of the young religious community soon began, incited by the clergy and condoned or ignored by the government. Condemned as apostates to Islam, more than twenty thousand Bábís were put to death in a few decades following 1844, many after fierce battles or horrific torture; tens of thousands of others were tortured, tormented, beggared, or banished for their allegiance to the new religion. The Báb Himself was executed in 1850 by a firing squad of 750 soldiers. This turmoil attracted the attention of the European press, which called for an end to the barbaric persecutions.

One of the first followers of the Báb was a wealthy Persian nobleman from the northern region of Núr, named Mírzá Ḥusayn-'Alí. Like the Báb, He had been distinguished since childhood for His attachment to God, precocious wisdom, charity, and seemingly innate understanding of religious scripture. After rising to prominence as a leader of the Bábí community, He was arrested in the summer of 1852, His home looted, His possessions seized, His family forced into hiding, and He was cast into a notorious dungeon in Tehran, chained to other Bábís and the worst criminals of the province. Every day one of the Bábís would be led out for torture and execution; the rest awaited their fate.

Mírzá Ḥusayn-'Alí later wrote that it was in this dungeon He received a revelation, in the form of a Heavenly vision and voice, announcing that He was the one foretold by the Báb, and that, impossible as it seemed at the time, through Him God would reveal teachings that would usher in a new spiritual and material age. Although another ten years would pass before He would make known His divine mandate, this sacred juncture, like the descent of the Dove of the Holy Spirit at Jesus's baptism, marks for Bahá'ís the shouldering of the mantle of divine authority by Mírzá

Ḥusayn-'Alí, and through that channel the beginning of the Bahá'í religion.*

In part by the intervention of the Russian ambassador, who warned that the execution of a person of His reputation would not be tolerated, Mírzá Ḥusayn-'Alí was exiled to Baghdad (then part of the Ottoman Empire), with His wife, two of His three small children, and a few close companions. The intent of the government was that His remoteness from the body of Bábí believers would end His influence. The harsh, three-month midwinter journey through the mountains of western Persia began in January 1853; food was in short supply and His children suffered frostbite that would affect them for the rest of their lives. This banishment would turn out to be the first of four successive exiles for the small band of Bábís, each taking them farther from the birthplace of the new religion.

Mírzá Ḥusayn-'Alí spent ten years in Baghdad as a prisoner of the Ottoman government. While not physically constrained, His movements were limited. Yet by a stream of correspondence and visits from Persian Bábís, He was able to revive the spirits of the disheartened followers of the Báb and keep them focused on their mission of preparing themselves for the coming advent of a greater revela-

---

* Although Siyyid 'Alí-Muḥammad (the Báb) and Mírzá Ḥusayn-'Alí never met, in retrospect many of the Báb's letters and actions indicate that He knew with certainty who was destined to be "Him whom God shall make manifest." The Báb's first act was to send His first and most intrepid disciple, Mullá Ḥusayn, to Tehran to give Mírzá Ḥusayn-'Alí the news of His advent. One of His last acts, shortly before His execution, was to send Mírzá Ḥusayn-'Alí the gift of a case containing His pens, seals, rings, and some important documents, the symbol of His revelation.

tion. During His years in Baghdad, He also wrote several books, one of which, the Kitáb-i-Íqán ("The Book of Certitude"), explains the nature of religious revelation and the search for religious truth. The contents of this book are important to understanding the second defining belief of the Bahá'ís, and will be examined in more detail in the next chapter, and again in chapter 5.

As His influence and prestige in Baghdad grew, the Persian ambassador pressured the Ottoman authorities to send Mírzá Husayn-'Alí even farther from Persia. In April 1863 plans were made for His exile to Constantinople (now Istanbul, Turkey). Mírzá Husayn-'Alí used the occasion of His departure from Baghdad to announce to a few of His closest followers what many of them already suspected, that He was "Him Whom God shall make manifest," the one foretold by the Báb nineteen years earlier. From this point forward, He would be known as *Bahá'u'lláh,* Arabic for "the Glory of God." This announcement, which occurred in an island garden in the Tigris River named Ridván (Paradise) on April 21, is celebrated by Bahá'ís (followers of Bahá'u'lláh) as their most important holy day. It was also at this time that Bahá'u'lláh set the tenor for this new religion by forbidding His followers the use of force in advancing or even defending their Faith, in spite of the persecutions they had suffered and the violent struggles they had been drawn into during the last nineteen years. Their only defense was to be their words. In a later document He writes: "Know thou that We have annulled the rule of the sword, as an aid to Our Cause, and substituted for it the power born of the utterance of men."[2]

Within a few years, the vast majority of Bábís came to wholeheartedly accept Bahá'u'lláh as the one for Whom the Báb had prepared them. The mission of the Báb was complete.

After only four months in Constantinople, Bahá'u'lláh and His followers were exiled once again in the dead of a harsh winter, this time to Adrianople (now Edirne) in eastern Turkey. It was there that Bahá'u'lláh publicly announced His mission, in a series of letters addressed to the civil and spiritual leaders of Asia, Europe, and America. The message of these letters is the foundation of the third defining belief and will be discussed in chapter 3.

Five years later (1868), again at the instigation of the Persian ambassador, the small band was forced to sell most of their belongings and was taken by a series of ships to Acre (Acco/'Akká) in Palestine, then the most remote and pestilential prison colony in the Ottoman Empire, situated a short distance from the present city of Haifa, Israel, near the foot of Mount Carmel. It was assumed that, sentenced to solitary confinement for life in Acre, Bahá'u'lláh and His religion would soon be extinguished.

This was not to be. During the next twenty-four years, until His death in 1892, Bahá'u'lláh continued to develop the foundations of the new religion in His writings. The most important of these is His book of laws, the Kitáb-i-Aqdas ("The Most Holy Book"), which includes a description of the nature of the new global society His followers are to construct. Discussion of these teachings will start in chapter 4.

The Center of the Covenant

In the Kitáb-i-Aqdas and the Kitáb-i-Ahd ("The Book of the Covenant"), also penned in Acre, Bahá'u'lláh appoints his eldest son, Abbas Effendi, as His successor, assigns him the title *Center of the Covenant,* and makes it clear that divine guidance will continue to flow through him:

O ye that dwell on earth! The religion of God is for love and unity; make it not the cause of enmity or dissension. . . . The Will of the divine Testator is this: It is incumbent upon the Aghsán [literally, branches; the relatives and descendants of Bahá'u'lláh*], the Afnán [literally, twigs; the relatives and descendants of The Báb] and My Kindred to turn, one and all, their faces towards the Most Mighty Branch [Abbas Effendi]. Consider that which We have revealed in Our Most Holy Book [Kitáb-i-Aqdas]: "When the ocean of My presence hath ebbed and the Book of My Revelation is ended, turn your faces toward Him Whom God hath purposed, Who hath branched from this Ancient Root." The object of this sacred verse is none other except the Most Mighty Branch. Thus have We graciously revealed unto you Our potent Will, and I am verily the Gracious, the All-Powerful.[3]

---

* Bahá'u'lláh's writings often contain phrases and allusions that have specific meanings well-known to Bahá'ís, but which will be unfamiliar to others. I am using square brackets to give the meaning or context whenever I feel it aids understanding. In this case, Bahá'u'lláh uses the metaphor of a tree to describe His family, with 'Abdu'l-Bahá described as "the Most Mighty Branch."

'Abbas Effendi, who took the title *Abdu'l-Bahá* ("Servant of Bahá") after his Father's passing, was nine years old when he first accompanied his father into exile in Baghdad, and he had served in the role of his father's deputy his entire adult life. His appointment to the position of leadership was accepted without hesitation by all but a few of his father's followers, and by the Ottoman authorities, who now targeted their hostility toward him.

The appointment of 'Abdu'l-Bahá as the new leader of the Bahá'í religion is the first chapter in the unfolding of the Bahá'í Covenant. In its simplest terms, this Covenant represents an agreement between Bahá'u'lláh and His followers that, in exchange for their fidelity (what Bahá'ís refer to as *firmness in the Covenant*), divine guidance would continue to flow to them through 'Abdu'l-Bahá, and in time through a unique system of institutions, which will be described shortly and again in chapter 6. Most significantly, this would protect the Bahá'í Faith from the internal dissension and division that typically follows the death of the founder of a new religion. It is an agreement unique in the world's religious history.

'Abdu'l-Bahá was given several specific responsibilities by his father. The most central was to be the authoritative interpreter of His writings. Bahá'ís place great weight on the written words of Bahá'u'lláh. Although historical accounts, recollections of conversations, anecdotes, and stories are invaluable and provide a special richness to an individual's faith, the body of Bahá'u'lláh's writings (over seventeen thousand documents) is regarded as pure religious revelation and the authoritative foundation of Bahá'í belief and practice. According to the pro-

visions of Bahá'u'lláh's Covenant, any question or contro-
versy arising over the meaning of any of His teachings was to
be referred to 'Abdu'l-Bahá, whose interpretations were to be
taken as binding. A letter from Bahá'u'lláh, known as the
Tablet of the Branch, makes it clear that He expects the Bahá'ís
to follow 'Abdu'l-Bahá's leadership. In a letter addressed to
'Abdu'l-Bahá, Bahá'u'lláh gives His son responsibility for
guiding all humanity:

> We have made Thee a shelter for all mankind, a shield
> unto all who are in heaven and on earth, a stronghold for
> whosoever hath believed in God, the Incomparable, the
> All-Knowing. God grant that through Thee He may pro-
> tect them, may enrich and sustain them, that He may
> inspire Thee with that which shall be a wellspring of
> wealth unto all created things, an ocean of bounty unto
> all men, and the dayspring of mercy unto all peoples.[4]

Another of the responsibilities given to 'Abdu'l-Bahá, and
in some ways the most miraculous, was that of being an
example for the Bahá'ís. 'Abdu'l-Bahá's life of tireless and
loving service, first to his father, then to the Bahá'ís, his
charitable works, his patience under extraordinary trials, and
his continual guidance and encouragement of the Bahá'ís,
together set a standard that all must strive to live up to.
Bahá'ís continue to study his life as well as his words for
inspiration on how to lead a "Bahá'í life" no matter what
the circumstances.

The Báb, Bahá'u'lláh, and 'Abdu'l-Bahá are the central figures of the Bahá'í religion. Bahá'ís regard them as holy per-

sons. The Báb and Bahá'u'lláh are regarded as *Manifestations of God,* equal in station to Christ, Muḥammad, Moses, and the founders of the other major world religions. While physically they are ordinary people, spiritually the Manifestations are completely different beings, created by God to be the recipients of a revelation for humanity, and given whatever spiritual powers and abilities they need to carry out their missions. (The idea of the Manifestation of God will be explored more fully in the next chapter.) Bahá'ís regard 'Abdu'l-Bahá as a person unique in religious history, with much of the authority and knowledge of the Manifestation, but working strictly in the context of his father's religion and Covenant. The writings of the Báb, Bahá'u'lláh, and 'Abdu'l-Bahá are regarded as the sacred texts of the Bahá'í Faith.

A prisoner since childhood, 'Abdu'l-Bahá was freed at the age of sixty-four following the overthrow of the Ottoman Empire in the Young Turk Revolution of 1908. He was then able to direct His efforts to the expansion of the Bahá'í Faith in Europe, North and South America, Africa, and Asia. 'Abdu'l-Bahá personally traveled to Egypt, Europe, and North America, speaking before hundreds of religious and civic organizations, and thousands of individual believers and Bahá'í groups. Later, when confined to the Holy Land by advancing age and the isolation imposed by World War I, he envisioned the spread of his father's religion around the globe and created systematic plans for the use of traveling teachers to develop Bahá'í communities in locales throughout the world. Some specific challenges He gave to the Bahá'ís of the United States are examined in chapters 7 and 14.

The Bahá'í Administrative Order

'Abdu'l-Bahá also left a written will in which he describes the administrative system the Bahá'ís are to build. This system consists of two complementary institutions: the Guardianship and the Universal House of Justice. The House of Justice, outlined in its basic features by Bahá'u'lláh in the Kitáb-i-Aqdas, is an elected institution responsible for, among other things, legislating on any matter not expressly covered in the writings of Bahá'u'lláh. The Guardianship, mentioned very briefly in Bahá'u'lláh's writings, is a hereditary institution responsible for interpretation of the meanings of the sacred texts. 'Abdu'l-Bahá appointed his grandson, Shoghi Effendi Rabbani, as the first Guardian of the Faith.* These institutions are promised divine guidance, and all Bahá'ís are to follow their leadership without hesitation. 'Abdu'l-Bahá states this in the strongest terms:

> The sacred and youthful branch [Shoghi Effendi], the guardian of the Cause of God, as well as the Universal House of Justice to be universally elected and established, are both under the care and protection of the Abhá Beauty [Bahá'u'lláh], under the shelter and unerring guidance of the Exalted One [the Báb] (may my life be offered up for them both). Whatsoever they decide is of God. Whoso obeyeth him not, neither obeyeth them, hath not obeyed God; whoso rebelleth against him and against them hath

---

* Bahá'ís often use "the Faith" (or "the Cause") to refer to their religion, and refer to Bahá'ís collectively as "the believers" or "the friends."

rebelled against God; whoso opposeth him hath opposed
God; whoso contendeth with them hath contended with
God; whoso disputeth with him hath disputed with God;
whoso denieth him hath denied God; whoso disbelieveth
in him hath disbelieved in God; whoso deviateth, separateth
himself and turneth aside from him hath in truth devi-
ated, separated himself and turned aside from God. May
the wrath, the fierce indignation, the vengeance of God
rest upon him! The mighty stronghold shall remain im-
pregnable and safe through obedience to him who is the
Guardian of the Cause of God.[5]

'Abdu'l-Bahá died in 1921 at the age of seventy-three.
After the reading of his Will and Testament, Shoghi Effendi,
who was then a student at Oxford, learned for the first time
of his appointment as Guardian. He left his studies to return to Palestine, and for the next thirty-six years used his
position as leader of the Bahá'í Faith to direct its spread to
most of the countries and territories of the world, to develop its administrative institutions, and to deepen every
Bahá'í's understanding of the fundamental teachings of the
Faith. He also began the systematic translation of the writings of the Báb, Bahá'u'lláh, and 'Abdu'l-Bahá into English
from their original Persian and Arabic.

The Universal House of Justice could not be formed until
the Bahá'ís in the majority of countries in the world had
elected the national governing bodies that would serve as
its electorate. Shoghi Effendi had initiated a plan of growth
and expansion, the Ten Year Crusade, to accomplish this
goal. The goals of the Ten Year Crusade, in turn, followed

directly from 'Abdu'l-Bahá's guidance laid out in the Tablets of the Divine Plan (see chapter 15). Despite Shoghi Effendi's unexpected death in 1957, leaving no heir to assume the position of Guardian,* the mechanism was in place to proceed with the election of the first Bahá'í Universal House of Justice. This election took place in 1963, on the one hundredth anniversary of Bahá'u'lláh's public announcement in Baghdad, at a gathering of the members of fifty-six Bahá'í National Assemblies. It was most probably the first democratic global election in history. Since then, the House of Justice has held the responsibility for ensuring the unity and progress of the Bahá'í religion. Bahá'ís value the books and letters of Shoghi Effendi and the House of Justice not as sacred writings, but still containing divine guidance, as promised by Bahá'u'lláh and 'Abdu'l-Bahá, for the audiences to whom they are addressed. Like the writings of the Báb, Bahá'u'lláh, and 'Abdu'l-Bahá, they are widely available to all in printed and electronic forms. They will be quoted extensively in this book.

The Bahá'í Covenant: A Spiritual Institution

Bahá'ís refer to this clear passing of authority, from Bahá'u'lláh to 'Abdu'l-Bahá to Shoghi Effendi and the Universal House of Justice, as the Bahá'í Covenant. It is regarded not just as a

---

* While many Bahá'ís took it for granted that their Faith would indefinitely have both elected and hereditary leadership, and were greatly dismayed for a time at the death of Shoghi Effendi, in retrospect some of Bahá'u'lláh's writings can be seen to anticipate the Universal House of Justice functioning without a person in the role of Guardian.

legal expedient or practical measure, but as a spiritual institution or force that is active in the world. This Covenant is the means for preserving the unity of the Bahá'í Faith, for protecting it from schism and keeping the Bahá'ís focused on their most important goals. Bahá'ís believe that God continues today to guide and assist those who align their actions with the leadership of the House of Justice.

My personal understanding of the Bahá'í Covenant is this: In the New Testament, it is clearly explained that God provides guidance to individuals through the Holy Spirit. The "gifts of the spirit" descend in ways that are outside of our ability to explain or predict: "To one there is given through the Spirit the message of wisdom, to another the message of knowledge by means of the same Spirit, to another faith by the same Spirit, to another gifts of healing by that one Spirit, to another miraculous powers, to another prophecy, to another distinguishing between spirits, to another speaking in different kinds of tongues, and to still another the interpretation of tongues. All these are the work of one and the same Spirit, and he gives them to each one, just as he determines."[6]

The guidance provided by the Holy Spirit is like the rain, which descends when and where God decrees, not always as we desire it. In this day, the same divine rain continues to fall, and individuals are still guided and inspired by the Holy Spirit. But now there is also a divine irrigation system, in the form of the Bahá'í Covenant, that directs the flow of God's heavenly guidance through a divinely designed and dependable channel. Both the Holy Spirit and the Bahá'í Covenant are instruments by which God continues to shower His guidance on humanity, directing the paths of His lovers and safeguarding His religion. If a Bahá'í thirsts for knowledge of God's plan and his place in it, he has the choice of waiting for the rain of inspiration or going to the river of guidance.*

Here then is the first defining belief of the Bahá'ís: God has provided for the unity and divine guidance of their religion through the unique spiritual institution of the Bahá'í Covenant. They proceed with confidence in Bahá'u'lláh's promise that God's guidance continues to flow through this institution to the House of Justice. This Covenant maintains the internal unity of the Bahá'í Faith. Even more, it makes possible the unity of purpose and action that are essential to the realization of the goals of the Faith. Without it, most of the unique Bahá'í practices described later in this book would be impossible.

None of the other world's great faiths started with an explicit, written covenant. Why does the Bahá'í Faith need one? This question goes to the heart of its unique mission.

All of God's religions begin with belief and faith; these are the foundation of His claim on man. But God does

---

* Things of the spirit are hard to put into concrete language, and religious texts often use analogies, metaphors, images, and parables in exploring and explaining spiritual realities. The danger, of course, is that people will forget that a metaphor is always open ended, and it becomes worshipped as a word-idol or ritualistic formula.

Hopefully, the analogy of a "divine irrigation system" helps to make more clear the idea that the Covenant is a "spiritual institution or force that is active in the world." This is my own analogy, but there are others used here borrowed from the Bahá'í writings and other sacred texts.

The Book of Revelation ends with St. John's vision of the City of God, the New Jerusalem, and the river of life, flowing from the Throne of God and the Lamb, down the middle of the street, watering the tree of life, the leaves of which are for the healing of the nations. I believe this river is a symbolic vision of the Covenant of Bahá'u'lláh.

not intend for His followers to merely have faith and belief and stop there. He expects them to live humble, reverent, and virtuous lives. The virtues that characterize this
life, as described by Bahá'u'lláh, are common to all the
great world faiths: "The virtues and attributes pertaining
unto God are all evident and manifest, and have been
mentioned and described in all the heavenly Books.
Among them are trustworthiness, truthfulness, purity of
heart while communing with God, forbearance, resigna-
tion to whatever the Almighty hath decreed, contentment
with the things His Will hath provided, patience, nay,
thankfulness in the midst of tribulation, and complete
reliance, in all circumstances, upon Him. These rank,
according to the estimate of God, among the highest and
most laudable of all acts."[7] Faith and belief, followed by
these virtues and qualities, have always been the hallmarks
of God's true followers. Trustworthiness, in particular, is
singled out by Bahá'u'lláh as a distinguishing characteristic of a holy life.

But even billions of people, each independently following the dictates above, would fail to fulfill God's plan for
today. Bahá'u'lláh adds another level of responsibility.
'Abdu'l-Bahá explains, "In every Dispensation [revealed re-
ligion] the light of Divine Guidance has been focused upon
one central theme. . . . In this wondrous Revelation, this
glorious century, the foundation of the Faith of God and
the distinguishing feature of His Law is the consciousness
of the Oneness of Mankind."[8]

Bahá'u'lláh calls on all people to come together in a new
civilization based on the consciousness of the oneness of hu-

manity. This is the purpose of His teachings, laws, and Covenant. The teachings of Bahá'u'lláh assign to the Bahá'ís the mission of building this civilization, and the unity created by the Covenant gives them the power to accomplish it.

'Abdu'l-Bahá makes it clear that behind the Covenant is a mighty spiritual force: "Today, the Lord of Hosts [God] is the defender of the Covenant, the forces of the Kingdom protect it, heavenly souls tender their services, and heavenly angels promulgate and spread it broadcast. If it is considered with insight, it will be seen that all the forces of the universe, in the last analysis serve the Covenant. In the future it shall be made evident and manifest."[9]

In the short history of the Bahá'í religion, the times of transition, at the passings of Bahá'u'lláh, 'Abdu'l-Bahá, and Shoghi Effendi, severely tested the firmness of many believers. A few, due perhaps to personal ambition, jealousy, ego, or confusion, chose to rebel against the clear requirements of the written Covenant and claim for themselves a special position of leadership. Although they caused turmoil and trouble for a time, especially for 'Abdu'l-Bahá and Shoghi Effendi, eventually their rebellions amounted to nothing. Bahá'ís regard the preservation of the unity of their Faith through these tests as proof of the spiritual power of Bahá'u'lláh's Covenant. 'Abdu'l-Bahá assures the Bahá'ís that attempts to break the Covenant will not succeed:

From the early days of creation down to the present time, throughout all the divine dispensations, such a firm and explicit Covenant hath not been entered upon. In view of this fact is it possible for this foam to remain on the surface of the ocean of the Covenant? No, by God! The violators are trampling upon their own dignity, are uprooting their own foundations and are proud at being upheld by flatterers who exert a great effort to shake the faith of feeble souls. But this action of theirs is of no consequence; it is a mirage and not water, foam and not the sea, mist and not a cloud, illusion and not reality. All this ye shall soon see.[10]

Bahá'u'lláh promises that He will continue to guide His followers through the institutions of the Center of the Covenant ('Abdu'l-Bahá), the Guardianship (Shoghi Effendi), and the Universal House of Justice. Nothing is more important to an individual Bahá'í than to remain faithful to and firm in this Covenant by accepting the channel of guidance it provides. While every Bahá'í is encouraged to study and think deeply about his religion and try to understand and reflect it in his daily life, Bahá'ís are warned never to confuse the authentic teachings of the Bahá'í Faith and the direction flowing through the channel of the Covenant with their own personal inspirations, interpretations, or the interpretations of others.

And nothing is more important to the Bahá'í community than preserving the unity of action made possible by the Covenant. This does not mean that every plan and program initiated by the Bahá'ís is divinely inspired or that it will automatically succeed. But the Bahá'í writings clearly state that when actions are undertaken with unity, mistakes will be readily apparent and easily corrected. The Bahá'í religion would be pointless (and impossible) without the spiritual institution of the Bahá'í Covenant.

2

God's Eternal Covenant

The Kitáb-i-Íqán ("The Book of Certitude") was written by Bahá'u'lláh in 1859, during the time of His exile in Baghdad. This book, composed in a period of two days and two nights,* was written for the uncle of the Báb, who had asked how to judge the truth of his nephew's teachings. It explains the nature of religious dispensations, why religions sometimes go astray, and how to seek religious certitude. A detailed analysis of all these topics is not the purpose of this book, but some points from the Kitáb-i-Íqán are important to the understanding of Bahá'í beliefs. Anyone interested in what Bahá'u'lláh teaches about God, humankind, and religion should carefully study the Kitáb-i-Íqán.

The Idea of the Manifestation of God

In this book, Bahá'u'lláh says that the infinite God is, in His essence, unknowable to the finite human mind; but the will of God and the attributes of God are made known from time to time throughout history. This happens when

---

* It is not really accurate to describe the writings of Bahá'u'lláh as being "composed." Shoghi Effendi explains, "All Divine Revelation seems to have been thrown out in flashes. The Prophets [Manifestations] never composed treatises. That is why in the Qur'án and our own Writings different subjects are so often included in one Tablet. It pulsates, so to speak. That is why it is 'Revelation.'" (Shoghi Effendi, *Unfolding Destiny,* p. 453.)

God sends His teachers to instruct humankind. Following Western religious tradition, Bahá'ís sometimes refer to these teachers as *Prophets*. But they do far more than prophesy. A more instructive title, used by Bahá'u'lláh, is *Manifestation of God.* God does not incarnate His *essence* in a human form, but He *manifests* Himself through these spiritually unique beings. These beings offer humanity perfect visions of God's qualities, such as holiness, glory, love, power, knowledge, grace, forgiveness, and justice. They renew the eternal teachings of all religions. In addition, and most important for the purpose of this book, they reveal the specific teachings required by humanity at that juncture in history. To experience them is to meet God.

In another place, Bahá'u'lláh provides this clear explanation of the importance of the Manifestation of God:

> The Prophets of God should be regarded as physicians whose task is to foster the well-being of the world and its peoples, that, through the spirit of oneness, they may heal the sickness of a divided humanity. To none is given the right to question their words or disparage their conduct, for they are the only ones who can claim to have understood the patient and to have correctly diagnosed its ailments. No man, however acute his perception, can ever hope to reach the heights which the wisdom and understanding of the Divine Physician have attained. Little wonder, then, if the treatment prescribed by the physician in this day should not be found to be identical with that which he prescribed before. How could it be otherwise when the ills affecting the sufferer neces-

sitate at every stage of his sickness a special remedy? In like manner, every time the Prophets of God have illumined the world with the resplendent radiance of the Day Star of Divine knowledge, they have invariably summoned its peoples to embrace the light of God through such means as best befitted the exigencies of the age in which they appeared. They were thus able to scatter the darkness of ignorance, and to shed upon the world the glory of their own knowledge. It is towards the inmost essence of these Prophets, therefore, that the eye of every man of discernment must be directed, inasmuch as their one and only purpose hath always been to guide the erring, and give peace to the afflicted.[1]

The human mind cannot fathom nor human language convey the relationship between God and His Manifestations. The Kitáb-i-Íqán uses the metaphor of a mirror. On the spiritual plane, each Manifestation of God is like a perfect mirror, reflecting the attributes of God the way a polished mirror perfectly reflects the light of the sun. If someone says "the sun is in the mirror" (as it appears to be), or "the sun is reflected by the mirror," he is speaking the truth either way. When the sun is reflected in two mirrors, it is correct to say that it is one sun, and that it is two. When no mirrors are present, the sun is not affected; it continues to shine whether its light is reflected or not. This is why Jesus can proclaim at one time that He is God, and at another that He is only God's obedient messenger, and both statements are completely true. Bahá'u'lláh explains that the Manifestations are all perfect mirrors, in a unique relationship with God, whereas the souls of ordinary men are like imperfect mirrors, fouled with dust and stains that they struggle to remove.

The Manifestations of God each carry out a preordained mission. Whether a Manifestation's ministry lasts for decades or just a few years, whether it attracts a handful of followers or millions, depends solely on God's plan and not on the Manifestation Himself. While they exhibit powers beyond those of ordinary people, by performing miracles, exhibiting innate knowledge of religious scriptures and teachings, foretelling the future and reading men's hearts— all of which are meant to open people's eyes and hearts and help them to believe—their most compelling and lasting power is revealed by the words they speak. These words are the force that changes the world. Invariably, these words alarm and threaten the entrenched religious establishment, which rises up to resist, persecute, and sometimes even kill, God's Messengers. God must love us very much to allow His Chosen Ones to be subjected to this certain brutality.

Bahá'u'lláh makes it clear that His followers should regard all the Manifestations of God as a single spiritual being appearing from time to time in different human bodies. Quoting the Koran, He cautions, "No distinction do We make between any of His Messengers" In another letter, Bahá'u'lláh explains the essential unity of the Manifestations of God, and that setting any one above the others is not allowed:

Know thou assuredly that the essence of all the Prophets of God is one and the same. Their unity is absolute. God, the Creator, saith: There is no distinction whatsoever among the Bearers of My Message. They all have but one purpose; their secret is the same secret. To prefer one in honor to another, to exalt certain ones above the rest, is in no wise to be permitted. Every true Prophet hath regarded His Message as fundamentally the same as the Revelation of every other Prophet gone before Him. If any man, therefore, should fail to comprehend this truth, and should consequently indulge in vain and unseemly language [honoring some of the Manifestations while disparaging others], no one whose sight is keen and whose understanding is enlightened would ever allow such idle talk to cause him to waver in his belief.

The measure of the revelation of the Prophets of God in this world, however, must differ. Each and every one of them hath been the Bearer of a distinct Message, and hath been commissioned to reveal Himself through specific acts. It is for this reason that they appear to vary in their greatness. Their Revelation may be likened unto the light of the moon that sheddeth its radiance upon the earth. Though every time it appeareth, it revealeth a fresh measure of its brightness, yet its inherent splendor can never diminish, nor can its light suffer extinction.*

---

* Bahá'u'lláh, *Gleanings,* no. 34. Take note of the phrase "commissioned to reveal Himself through specific acts." My understanding is that sometimes it seems that the Manifestations are sent by God on missions doomed to earthly failure. Christ first offered salvation to the Jews and told His disciples not to teach the Gentiles and Samaritans (Matthew 10:5–6). Only after this offer was rejected did He call on His disciples to take the Gospel to all peoples. Similarly, Bahá'u'lláh offered a path to peace to the kings and rulers of the world (see chapter 3); after this call was rejected, He gave the job of building peace to His followers (see chapter 4). Certainly God knew these missions would fail and that His Chosen Ones would suffer greatly for even attempting them. These missions are some of the "specific acts" through which the Manifestations are commissioned to reveal themselves.

Bahá'u'lláh affirms that the Manifestations of God know
far more than they are allowed to reveal, because humanity
can only respond to a certain portion at a given time. They
are like the teachers in a grade school. The lower grade teacher
has a complete understanding of higher mathematics, but it
is in the best interests of his students to teach only the arith-
metic they can grasp. In one grade children learn how to
count and add; they cannot imagine anything more complex. In the next they learn about subtraction, and soon nega-
tive numbers appear. The next teacher introduces division;
the students learn there are fractions between the numbers
they know, and then discover irrational numbers. In this way,
each teacher unfolds a new level of complexity and richness,
building on the lessons learned before, without in any way
demeaning the earlier teachers or their lessons.

The Paradigm of Progressive Revelation

Throughout history, the Manifestations have revealed God's
plan through a never-ending series of religions, each adapted
to the capacity of its audience, progressively increasing
humanity's understanding of God and His will. In strong
language, Bahá'u'lláh rejects the notion that God's revelation
can ever cease:

> Can one of sane mind ever seriously imagine that, in view
> of certain words the meaning of which he cannot com-
> prehend, the portal of God's infinite guidance can ever be
> closed in the face of men? Can he ever conceive for these
> Divine Luminaries, these resplendent Lights [the Mani-
> festations of God] either a beginning or an end? What

outpouring flood can compare with the stream of His all-embracing grace and what blessing can excel the evidences of so great and pervasive a mercy? . . . Such hath been God's method continued from everlasting to everlasting.[2]

Bahá'ís refer to this process, by which God provides regular guidance to humanity through these beings called Manifestations, as *progressive revelation*. Its roots are implicit in the way Muslims see their religion as a renewal of Christianity, Christians see their faith as the fulfillment of Judaism, and Jews see the Law of Moses as a completion of the covenant God made with Abraham. Progressive revelation is the second distinctive belief of the Bahá'ís. It reassures them that God *has always* and *will always* love *all* humanity and will *never* abandon us. God always keeps His promises. And He does it by sending these Manifestations to renew His eternal teachings, inspire the pure in heart and catalyze "an ever-advancing civilization."* These special beings can only be regarded as the supreme evidences of God's love for humanity. They are the ultimate proof of the existence and goodness of God.

Many devoutly religious people have difficulty accepting the idea of progressive revelation. Muḥammad wrote that He is "the seal of the prophets."[3] Many Muslims interpret this verse of the Koran literally as meaning there cannot be another Prophet (Manifestation) after Muḥammad, at least until "the end of the age," an interpretation that was the basis for their rejection and persecution of the Báb and Bahá'u'lláh and their followers. These are the "certain words the mean-

---

* "All men have been created to carry forward an ever-advancing civilization." (Bahá'u'lláh, *Gleanings,* no. 109.2.)

ing of which he cannot comprehend" mentioned in the quote above. Bahá'u'lláh rejects this interpretation, pointing out that Muḥammad also said He was the first Prophet, and at the same time, all the Prophets.*

This same pattern—followers of a religion rejecting the new Manifestation—is repeated throughout religious history. Even if people are able to acknowledge on some level the beauty and value of the world's great religious systems, they resist the idea that they are in some way "progressive," or that God has more to tell us. Since they cannot imagine a revelation greater, more beautiful or profound than the one they know and love, they imagine instead that divine revelation has forever ceased, that the last thing God said is the final truth and can never be expanded or superseded even by a more complete and broader truth. Any claim of a new revelation is by definition a threat to their belief system, even though it affirms the divine origin of their religion and the divine reality of their teacher, and adds new depth and beauty to what they already believe.

---

* See Bahá'u'lláh, Kitáb-i-Íqán, ¶161–72. I am tempted at this point to venture into some amateur theology. The Manifestations of God (plural) we experience historically (e.g., Moses, Jesus, Muḥammad, Bahá'u'lláh) are instances/realizations/incarnations/manifestations of an eternal divine Being, *the* Manifestation of God (singular). Muḥammad says He is the first Prophet and the last Prophet and all those in between; in other words, He is eternal. Christ was expressing this same truth when he said, "Before Abraham was born, I am!" (John 8:58) Clearly He was not speaking of His physical body here (although it was His body that was stoned for speaking these words). I understand this eternal Being to be what Christians refer to as "the Son of God," "the Word" which is "made flesh," in this physical world, a part of the Trinity, eternal and unchanging. The reality of this divine being is far beyond mortal comprehension and its description beyond the limits of human language.

To accept the truth of progressive revelation is to accept that God's plan for this world is still unfolding. According to Bahá'u'lláh, God has promised never to leave humanity without guidance. The guidance sent through the Manifestations of God has occurred from the beginning of human time, and will continue forever. Each of these Prophets of God, despite suffering rejection and intense persecution from the religious establishment of the day, has made it clear that He is the fulfillment of the prophecies of the prior Prophets, and prophesies a time when another divine teacher will appear. Bahá'ís refer to this promise as the "Greater Covenant" to distinguish it from the specific covenants that are made between a particular Manifestation and His followers. But at another level, these two covenants are really the same: God promises to send humanity further guidance, in exchange for which we promise to act on the guidance given so far and to watch for the next teacher.

Because they see the world's faiths as unfolding expressions of God's love and purpose for all humankind, Bahá'ís see religion not just as another static aspect or dimension of secular human history, but as its fundamental driving current. Beneath the superficial history of civilizations, cultures, and economies rising and falling and often clashing with each other, there is the recurring pattern of redemptive spiritual energy released by the Manifestations of God, launching the great religious systems of the world and inspiring individuals to create beauty, to seek truth and knowledge, and to increase love and establish justice. These revelations are not in any sense independent of each other. Each confirms the validity of its predecessors, builds upon

them and gives the teachings necessary for that day, and
promises another divine teacher in the fullness of time.* At
the time of its birth, every new religion is seen as extreme
and dangerous to established institutions and patterns of
life, because it *is* dangerous. Each new Manifestation changes
the practices and social laws of God's religion to suit the
requirements of the age in which He has appeared. It is not
for man to challenge God on His actions. Bahá'u'lláh writes,

> Blessed is the man that hath acknowledged his belief in
> God and in His signs, and recognized that "He shall not
> be asked of His doings." Such a recognition hath been
> made by God the ornament of every belief, and its very
> foundation. Upon it must depend the acceptance of ev-
> ery goodly deed. Fasten your eyes upon it, that haply the
> whisperings of the rebellious may not cause you to slip.
>
> Were He to decree as lawful the thing which from time
> immemorial had been forbidden, and forbid that which
> had, at all times, been regarded as lawful, to none is given
> the right to question His authority. . . . Whoso hath not
> recognized this sublime and fundamental verity, and hath
> failed to attain this most exalted station, the winds of doubt
> will agitate him, and the sayings of the infidels will dis-
> tract his soul. He that hath acknowledged this principle
> will be endowed with the most perfect constancy.[4]

---

* The Báb says this simply and directly, as is His style: "The Lord of the
universe hath never raised up a prophet nor hath He sent down a Book [teach-
ings] unless He hath established His covenant with all men, calling for their
acceptance of the next Revelation and of the next Book; inasmuch as the
outpourings of His bounty are ceaseless and without limit." (The Báb, *Selections from the Writings of the Báb*, no. 3:12.2.)

But there is another dimension of progressive revelation that I understand to be even more fundamental than changes to the religious laws and practices. Bahá'u'lláh claims that every time God sends a Manifestation, there are profound changes in the unseen spiritual world, changes that, in reality, are the reason for changes in the outward form of religion. Each Manifestation releases a new spiritual capacity and energy into the world. Basic spiritual truths, assumed by many to be eternal and unchanging, are expanded, amended, and revised. God can do this, because He is the creator of the spiritual world. This is the expression of His redemptive love and grace. The new beliefs and practices that are the focus of this book are only reflections of new spiritual realities originating with God. Exploration of this dimension will resume in chapter 4.

The Kitáb-i-Íqán explains how the prophecies contained in the holy books, although often couched in the language of the material world, are really about the spiritual world. For example, the New Testament prophecy that, at the time of Christ's return, "The stars shall fall from the sky,"[5] may be fulfilled by a literal star fall (a meteor shower, for example). But there will also be a spiritual fulfillment that is more fundamental. In this case, Bahá'u'lláh explains that the stars refer to the religious leaders and divine teachings that in the past served as true guides for humankind. At the time of Christ's return, these stars will fail to provide direction: "Hence, it is clear and manifest that by the words 'the sun shall be darkened, and the moon shall not give her light, and the stars shall fall from heaven' is intended the waywardness of the divines, and the annulment of laws firmly established by divine Revelation, all of which, in symbolic

35

language, have been foreshadowed by the Manifestation of God."[6] Bahá'u'lláh makes it clear that the religion originates in the spiritual worlds of God and its teachings cannot be understood by strictly material or practical interpretations.*

The spiritual renewal and advancement that accompany the appearance of a new Manifestation of God is the catalyst to the rise of great civilizations and the cause of progress in the material worlds of science, art, and human relationships:

> The light which these souls [the Manifestations of God] radiate is responsible for the progress of the world and the advancement of its peoples. They are like unto leaven which leaveneth the world of being, and constitute the animating force through which the arts and wonders of the world are made manifest. Through them the clouds rain their bounty upon men, and the earth bringeth forth its fruits. All things must needs have a cause, a motive power, an animating principle. These souls and symbols of detachment have provided, and will continue to provide, the supreme moving impulse in the world of being.[7]

---

* "For I do not speak of my own accord, but the Father who sent me commanded me what to say and how to say it. I know that his command leads to eternal life. So whatever I say is just what the Father has told me to say." (John 12:49–50.)

Social scientists and historians may attempt to interpret the genesis of a religion as the creation of a charismatic human being in response to his socio-political milieu. Bahá'u'lláh rejects this narrowly secular perspective. While the responses of people to this event may be studied historically, the founder of the faith, the Manifestation of God, is not creating but *revealing* a new religion. He does not even have free will in the matter, at least as we understand free will. And while the time and place provide a stage and backdrop for the delivery of God's message, portions of it may be meant for audiences in other times and places that only God can see.

No doubt future scholars will investigate these claims and attempt to unravel the effects that the coming of God's holy teachers have had on great leaps forward in civilization, philosophy, science, and the arts.

Man's religious life needs periodic renewal as well. Bahá'u'lláh often uses the rose as a symbol of man's pure love for God; He says, "In the garden of thy heart plant naught but the rose of love."[8] Yet over the centuries, the religious life of a people becomes stunted and constrained, and the rose of love finds itself transplanted to a pot and put on a shelf, to be brought out only on socially approved and ceremonial occasions, while man's heart is given over to other loves, broad visions are replaced by preoccupation with narrow issues, and religion is left "having a form of godliness, but denying its power."[9] Like a living plant so confined, religion will first become distorted into fanaticism as it struggles to escape, then wither and die and eventually become a dried flower, still symbolic but brittle and impotent.

The Manifestations come to release God's religion from this fate. Replanting the rose of love in the sunshine, they permit it to grow and release its potential for good and beauty. God is again staking his claim to the human heart, all of it. This is the second defining belief of the Bahá'ís: God has eternally renewed His spiritual creation and given to humanity, through the divine Manifestations, the guidance it needs to advance according to His plan. Today, Bahá'ís believe He has done this once again through the revelation of Bahá'u'lláh. Religion is being let out of its confinement to reestablish its central role in the life and society of all peoples.

Bahá'u'lláh states explicitly in the Kitáb-i-Aqdas that another Manifestation will be sent by God sometime after a full one thousand years, and warns His followers not to treat that One the way He was treated. There is no possible way for a Bahá'í to claim, now or in the future, that God's revelation has culminated in Bahá'u'lláh.

Understanding the idea of the Manifestation of God and recognizing the truth and power of progressive revelation will give the seeker new insights into the meaning of the religious scriptures of the past. Many teachings that before seemed unimportant gain new significance, and some teachings that were very confusing now make sense. Once one accepts that God has always loved all people without distinction, it is hard to return to a belief that some are His chosen people and others are not.

The Bahá'í writings do not contain any list or catalog of the Manifestations of God. The founders of all the great religions of the East and West are specifically mentioned: Adam,* Krishna, Buddha, Zoroaster, Abraham, Moses, Christ, and Muḥammad, along with the Báb and Bahá'u'lláh. But the statement of Bahá'u'lláh, quoted above, that in the appearance of the Manifestations there is neither "a beginning or an end," I understand to mean that God has sent divine Messengers to every region and people of the planet, and has done so for thousands of years, long before the records

---

* Islam has a different understanding of the station of Adam than does Christianity. To Muslims, He represents a symbolic first Prophet (Manifestation) and the beginning of a historical cycle in which God communicates to man through these Prophets. The Bahá'í writings also support this view. See, for example, *Gleanings*, no. 87.

of history, "from everlasting to everlasting." Although the Manifestations listed here have appeared in the form of men, the Bahá'í writings state clearly that gender is an attribute of the physical world and that God, the Manifestations (in their spiritual essence), and the human soul are neither male nor female. Unfortunately, the English language makes it awkward to refer to beings, spiritual or otherwise, without attaching a gender.*

How to Seek God

The Kitáb-i-Íqán deals extensively with the search for religious truth and certainty. The claims of the Báb and Bahá'u'lláh, that they are divine Messengers with new teachings for humanity, are about the most audacious words a person can speak. How does a seeker after religious truth decide whether a Messenger and His message are truly divine in origin?

The search for religious certainty at this level is an extremely personal and private pursuit. To begin with, no one should ever feel that she is not smart enough, not wise enough, or not spiritual enough to seek God. Nor should anyone ever judge that another is unworthy or unable to respond to God's message. The capacity to recognize God through His Manifestations is innate within every person's soul. She just needs to seek earnestly; the All-Merciful God

---

* Arabic and Farsi, the original languages of the Bahá'í writings, allow for nongendered references to God. Bahá'u'lláh writes of the Manifestations as "the divine Beauty . . . appear[ing] in the form of the human temple." (Kitáb-i-Íqán, ¶74).

will do the rest. As Christ said, "Ask and it will be given to you; seek and you will find; knock and the door will be opened."[10] Bahá'u'lláh asserts that everyone can seek and find God:

He [God] hath endowed every soul with the capacity to recognize the signs of God. How could He, otherwise, have fulfilled His testimony unto men [God's eternal covenant], if ye be of them that ponder His Cause in their hearts. He will never deal unjustly with anyone, neither will He task a soul beyond its power. He, verily, is the Compassionate, the All-Merciful.

Say: So great is the glory of the Cause of God that even the blind can perceive it, how much more they whose sight is sharp, whose vision is pure.[11]

In the beginning of the Kitáb-i-Íqán, Bahá'u'lláh says that the first step in this search is to become detached from the material world and the ideas of humanity:

No man shall attain the shores of the ocean of true understanding except he be detached from all that is in heaven and on earth. . . . The essence of these words is this: they that tread the path of faith, they that thirst for the wine of certitude, must cleanse themselves of all that is earthly—their ears from idle talk, their minds from vain imaginings, their hearts from worldly affections, their eyes from that which perisheth. They should put their trust in God, and, holding fast unto Him, follow in His way. Then will they be made worthy of the effulgent glories of the sun of divine knowledge and understanding, and become the recipients of a grace that is infinite and unseen.[12]

In particular, people should not let man-made religious doctrines sway them in their search. Bahá'u'lláh uses the history of the dispensations of Moses, Christ, and Muḥammad to investigate why the Manifestations of God have always been rejected and persecuted by the people they were sent to save. One reason is that the religious leaders of the day, either through ignorance or love of power, have refused to let people listen to their message:

> Leaders of religion, in every age, have hindered their people from attaining the shores of eternal salvation [recognition of the new Manifestation], inasmuch as they held the reins of authority in their mighty grasp. Some for the lust of leadership, others through want of knowledge and understanding, have been the cause of the deprivation of the people. By their sanction and authority, every Prophet of God hath drunk from the chalice of sacrifice, and winged His flight unto the heights of glory. What unspeakable cruelties they that have occupied the seats of authority and learning have inflicted upon the true Monarchs of the world, those Gems of divine virtue! Content with a transitory dominion, they have deprived themselves of an everlasting sovereignty.
>
> . . . The denials and protestations of these leaders of religion have, in the main, been due to their lack of knowledge and understanding. Those words uttered by the Revealers of the beauty of the one true God, setting

forth the signs that should herald the advent of the Manifestation to come, they never understood nor fathomed.
Hence they raised the standard of revolt, and stirred up
mischief and sedition.[13]

Anyone can *claim* to be the bearer of a message from
God. How can the seeker distinguish a true divine messenger from false prophets, the deluded and charlatans of various motives? In the Kitáb-i-Íqán and subsequent works,
Bahá'u'lláh explains that a spiritually discerning person can
recognize a Manifestation of God by three "proofs." This is
my understanding of these writings: The first proof is "His
own Self," meaning that those who are fortunate enough to
meet Him will know He is who He claims He is. The histories of the births of the great religions reveal that, time and
again, people were magnetically attracted to these persons
and recognized them as God's Messengers, even though they
may not have comprehended their teachings on an intellectual level. Christ had only to say "follow me" and the disciples followed. About those who attain the presence of a
Manifestation and recognize His station, the Báb says,
"There is no paradise more wondrous for any soul than to
be exposed to God's Manifestation in His Day, to hear His
verses and believe in them, to attain His presence, which is
naught but the presence of God, to sail upon the sea of the
heavenly kingdom of His good-pleasure, and to partake of
the choice fruits of the paradise of His divine Oneness."[14]

The second proof is that those who read or hear His teachings will know they are from God, not man. This is the
proof of "The Book," and is the strongest proof, since the

soul of every person is capable recognizing the voice of God when they hear it. The scriptures of a faith are more than just a collection of its teachings; through them you can discern that divine voice and follow it to certitude. This is why these scriptures continue to be held in such reverence by their followers, even after some of their teachings seem to lose practical relevance.

And the third proof is that His followers are transformed by His teachings. In retrospect, we can see that the humble teachings of these "Divine Physicians" were able to unite age-old enemies in great civilizations, inspiring their followers to seek knowledge, to create justice, to add beauty to the world, and to multiply love.

If you inquire into the relatively brief history of the Bahá'í religion, you will find stories of many people who found the answer to their quest for certainty by meeting the persons of the Báb, Bahá'u'lláh, or 'Abdu'l-Bahá. It is still possible to meet them today by reading the stories of their lives and learning how they suffered to bring their message of peace built on unity and justice. This is the first proof and is sufficient for many. There are places in the world with large and thriving Bahá'í communities where many people are attracted by the character, behavior, and actions of the Bahá'ís. Even where the Bahá'ís are fewer in number, people are often attracted to the Bahá'í Faith because they detect something special in the followers of Bahá'u'lláh. This is the third proof in action. But the surest means to judge the claim of Bahá'u'lláh is to prepare one's spirit through prayer and detachment, then to listen to His words and read His book, and to judge for oneself whether or not it is from God. For

the spiritual person, to fulfill one's quest for certitude by recognizing the Manifestation of God is the greatest joy that
can be experienced. This topic will be revisited in chapter 5.

3

The Oneness of Humankind
Will Be Established

When the teachings and beliefs that distinguish the Bahá'ís from the followers of other faiths are inventoried, one of the most remarkable is that Bahá'ís share a single, clear vision of the future, and they believe they have a central role in realizing this vision.

At the Threshold of a New Age

Despite great strides in the natural and human sciences, medicine, technology, and human rights, much of humanity's recent history has been a litany of war, genocide, terrorism, tyranny, racism, dehumanizing ideologies and pseudo-sciences, psychological and social chaos, seemingly intractable poverty, and unbridled avarice. It would seem that no reasonable person can follow the news and be convinced that the future will be significantly different. Yet the Bahá'ís believe, contrary to any lesson history teaches, that humanity is at the threshold of an age of peace, true liberty, democracy, tolerance, prosperity, and economic and social justice. This coming age will not be just a short intermission in an ongoing tragedy, but a new era lasting tens of thousands of years.

Bahá'u'lláh frequently uses metaphors and parables from the natural world, such as the processes of birth and death, growth and development, or sickness and health, to explain spiritual truths. In describing the state of the world today, Bahá'u'lláh makes a metaphor of the process of birth, in which a new creation comes from old: "The whole earth is now in a state of pregnancy, the day is approaching when it will have yielded its noblest fruits, when from it will have sprung forth the loftiest trees, the most enchanting blossoms, the most heavenly blessings."[1]

At birth, a baby is forced, no doubt against its instincts, from a warm, comfortable, familiar environment—the only world it has ever known—to a frightening and confusing place, full of cold winds, harsh sounds, and bright lights. Yet it is only in this new world that it can realize its potential and begin to put to use the hands and feet, eyes and ears and brain that it was developing in the womb. Bahá'u'lláh says this is the state of the world today. All humanity is being forced into a new reality, frightening in the short term but glorious in the long term. It has developed as far as it can in a world divided and warring. To go further, humanity must have unity, justice, and peace.

One of the most frequently encountered metaphors in the Bahá'í writings, used by Bahá'u'lláh, 'Abdu'l-Bahá, Shoghi Effendi, and now by the Universal House of Justice, is that of the stages of human maturation. Collectively, humanity has left its childhood and entered adolescence; this is referred to as humankind's "coming of age." Humanity is beginning to have adult thoughts mixed in with its childish thoughts, and is starting to comprehend wider truths and see broader visions. Yet it still exhibits childlike patterns of behavior on a regular basis. In the words of Shoghi Effendi, "The ages of its infancy and childhood are past, never again to return, while the Great Age, the consummation of all ages, which must signalize the coming of age of the entire human race, is yet to come."[2]

Peace Will be Achieved

The crowning achievement of this coming age of maturity will be a lasting peace among all nations. Lives and resources now pouring into war and preparation for war will be freed to serve higher ends. Supporting peace will be a world parliament and tribunal, education for all children, a universal language, and an economy organized for the benefit of all. The current human institutions and programs that promote peace (e.g., the United Nations), as valuable and necessary as they are at present, by themselves cannot create the lasting peace envisaged by the Bahá'í writings. The true foundation of that peace, what Bahá'u'lláh calls "the Most Great Peace," will be the realization of the spiritual, physical, and organic oneness of humanity. A single sentence from Bahá'u'lláh captures the relationship between peace and unity: "The well-being of mankind, its peace and security, are unattainable unless and until its unity is firmly established."[3]

This is the kernel of the Bahá'í understanding of the world situation, and the foundation of its plan for world salvation. Bahá'ís intend to firmly establish the unity of humankind, thereby creating the foundation on which true peace and well-being can be based. That peace can and must be achieved at this time is the third defining belief of the Bahá'í religion. It gives Bahá'ís a single overriding focus and mission, and allows them to remain undistracted and undismayed by the chaos of the world.

The rest of the above quotation from Shoghi Effendi clarifies the Bahá'í understanding of this time in human history:

> The ages of its infancy and childhood are past, never again to return, while the Great Age, the consummation of all ages, which must signalize the coming of age of the entire human race, is yet to come. The convulsions of this transitional and most turbulent period in the annals of humanity are the essential prerequisites, and herald the inevitable approach, of that Age of Ages, "the time of the end," in which the folly and tumult of strife that has, since the dawn of history, blackened the annals of mankind, will have been finally transmuted into the wisdom and the tranquility of an undisturbed, a universal, and lasting peace, in which the discord and separation of the children of men will have given way to the worldwide reconciliation, and the complete unification of the divers elements that constitute human society.[4]

In another place Shoghi Effendi connects the chaos of the present to the outmoded system of competing, sovereign states:

> Unification of the whole of mankind is the hall-mark of the stage which human society is now approaching. Unity

of family, of tribe, of city-state, and nation have been successively attempted and fully established. World unity is the goal towards which a harassed humanity is striving. Nation-building has come to an end. The anarchy inherent in state sovereignty is moving towards a climax. A world, growing to maturity, must abandon this fetish, recognize the oneness and wholeness of human relationships, and establish once for all the machinery that can best incarnate this fundamental principle of its life.[5]

Peace among nations is the hallmark of the age of maturity foretold by Bahá'u'lláh. This peace is not to be equated with some utopian dreamworld, where there are never any problems or disagreements, but one in which international disputes are settled by discussion, law, and justice without resorting to war. Bahá'u'lláh acknowledges that nations will still require police and other forces to deter crime and maintain order within their borders, and that they must be ready to collectively thwart the aggression of one nation against another. They will be in a federated relationship, with a portion of their sovereignty, including the right to unilaterally start a conflict, ceded to international bodies. It is daily becoming more apparent that many of the world's problems will only yield to a new approach based on international agreement and cooperation rather than power, contention, and belligerence. The environment, education, economic development, health promotion, and human rights are all areas where progress is stymied when every nation clings to its own standards and narrow interests.

To connect this theme to the idea of God's greater covenant from the last chapter, Bahá'u'lláh, like the Manifestations gone before, reaffirms and reinforces the basic spiritual teachings of all the major religions. And like them, He adds social teachings ideally suited to addressing the problems of the age. At the heart of Bahá'u'lláh's social teachings is the imperative of the unity of humankind. Lack of true unity, He says, is the root cause of the major ills of the world; until it is achieved, no real progress is possible. Creating this unity is the purpose of Bahá'u'lláh's religion. All of the Bahá'í teachings examined in the coming chapters, in one way or another, support this imperative of world unity.

A Twofold Process at Work

So Bahá'ís believe, contrary to anything history and experience teaches, that an era of true peace is certain to arrive, and they will provide its foundation by creating unity among nations and peoples. Before exploring how they intend to do this (which is essentially the task of the rest of this book), it is instructive to ask, how long will it take for humanity to reach the stage of maturity predicted by Bahá'u'lláh, and when will this promised peace be established.

Throughout His ministry, but particularly during His period of exile in Adrianople (1864–68), Bahá'u'lláh audaciously directed letters to the kings and rulers of the Middle East, Europe, and America, calling on them to abandon their ways of tyranny, oppression, and aggression, and instead to rule with justice and come together to settle their disputes peacefully, for the pleasure of God, their own glory and the benefit of their subjects.* These letters make it clear that Bahá'u'lláh places responsibility for the world's turmoil squarely on these leaders, and that He viewed that juncture in history as a window of opportunity during which a lasting peace could be established "from the top down." But this call was ignored or rejected, and the intervening years have seen successive, needless wars in which tens of millions have perished, great cities were destroyed, empires brought to collapse, and rich nations made destitute.

After each of the last century's terrible wars, international movements, and institutions for peace were initiated. 'Abdu'l-Bahá frequently addressed peace organizations during his Western travels, corresponded with institutions such as the Central Organization for a Durable Peace at The Hague, and met with numerous peace workers, encouraging and praising their work, while at the same time making it clear that peace must be built on spiritual unity. During his years as Guardian, Shoghi Effendi was quick to develop formal relationships between the Bahá'í Faith and the League of Nations, and later with the United Nations. The relationship of the Bahá'ís with the UN continues to develop and will be discussed in chapter 10.

Through their elected institutions (the Universal House of Justice and the National Spiritual Assemblies), Bahá'ís are again calling the nations of the world to peace. The House of Justice renewed this call in 1985 when it published *The*

---

* The English translations of several of these letters have been published in Bahá'u'lláh, *Summons of the Lord of Hosts* (Haifa: Bahá'í World Center, 2002).

Promise of World Peace. This document begins with this pronouncement: "The Great Peace towards which people of good will throughout the centuries have inclined their hearts, of which seers and poets for countless generations have expressed their vision, and for which from age to age the sacred scriptures of mankind have constantly held the promise, is now at long last within the reach of the nations."[6]

The Promise of World Peace should be read by anyone who wants to know what the Bahá'í Faith teaches about the state of the world. Peace is within the reach of the nations, whenever they gather the collective will to grasp it; the alternatives include a worst-case scenario, in which "unimaginable horrors" gradually exhaust the nations, until they have no recourse but to accept peace: "Whether peace is to be reached only after unimaginable horrors precipitated by humanity's stubborn clinging to old patterns of behavior, or is to be embraced now by an act of consultative will, is the choice before all who inhabit the earth. At this critical juncture when the intractable problems confronting nations have been fused into one common concern for the whole world, failure to stem the tide of conflict and disorder would be unconscionably irresponsible."[7]

There is no indication in the Bahá'í writings as to how long this process might take. In fact, it depends to some extent on the Bahá'ís themselves, on how rapidly they progress on their appointed mission and spread the foundation of unity. Shoghi Effendi writes that a twofold process is at work, in which the obstacles to peace are torn down as the Bahá'í program of unity spreads and strengthens:

A twofold process . . . can be distinguished, each tend-
ing, in its own way and with an accelerated momentum,
to bring to a climax the forces that are transforming the
face of our planet. The first is essentially an integrating
process, while the second is fundamentally disruptive.
The former, as it steadily evolves, unfolds a System which
may well serve as a pattern for that world polity towards
which a strangely-disordered world is continually advancing; while the latter, as its disintegrating influence deep-
ens, tends to tear down, with increasing violence, the
antiquated barriers that seek to block humanity's progress
towards its destined goal. The constructive process stands
associated with the nascent Faith of Bahá'u'lláh, and is
the harbinger of the New World Order that Faith must
erelong establish. The destructive forces that characterize the other should be identified with a civilization that
has refused to answer to the expectation of a new age,
and is consequently falling into chaos and decline.[8]

In this worst-case scenario, where the nations and institutions of the world continue to cling to their outmoded world
view, peace will have to be built from the ground up, by
building unity among people as the age-old obstacles to
peace are (sometimes violently) removed. The integrating
process, the job of building unity, is the work of the Bahá'ís.

The Meaning of Unity

The vast majority of Bahá'u'lláh's spiritual, social, and moral
teachings are related to creating, maintaining, and reinforc-

53

ing unity within families, among the Bahá'ís themselves, between Bahá'ís and the members of other faith communities, between societies and the natural world, and between the nations and peoples of the earth. But what do Bahá'ís really mean by the word *unity?* The foundation of unity is spiritual; it begins when people see themselves and others, first and foremost, as connected members of one human family: "World order can be founded only on an unshakable consciousness of the oneness of mankind, a spiritual truth that all the human sciences confirm. Anthropology, physiology, psychology, recognize only one human species, albeit infinitely varied in the secondary aspects of life. Recognition of this truth requires abandonment of prejudice—prejudice of every kind—race, class, color, creed, nation, sex, degree of material civilization, everything which enables people to consider themselves superior to others."[9]

But the recognition of the oneness of humanity is only the foundation. No amount of love and good feelings can, by themselves, solve the world's problems; a world with only love would soon decline into anarchy. Love must be followed by collective actions—actions that lead to order, peace, justice, and prosperity. How is this possible? These paragraphs from the House of Justice deserve close attention:

> For unity to exist among human beings—at even the simplest level—two fundamental conditions must pertain. Those involved must first of all be in some agreement about the nature of reality as it affects their relationships with one another and with the phenomenal

world. They must, secondly, give assent to some recognized and authoritative means by which decisions will be taken that affect their association with one another and that determine their collective goals.

Unity is not, that is, merely a condition resulting from a sense of mutual goodwill and common purpose, however profound and sincerely held such sentiments may be, any more than an organism is a product of some fortuitous and amorphous association of various elements. Unity is a phenomenon of creative power, whose existence becomes apparent through the effects that collective action produces and whose absence is betrayed by the impotence of such efforts.[10]

Unity is thus revealed through action. It starts with a recognition of the fundamental oneness of humanity (i.e., love), but then requires something in addition to love. United people will come together and agree on a system for making decisions and taking collective action. They will agree in advance to support the decisions that are made and the actions that are taken. This is certainly the hard part of unity, the part that requires maturity at both individual and collective scales. The ideal system will require procedures, rules and institutions, must be fair and just (both in perception and reality), and must wield authority and expect compliance. An analogy might be musical harmony: the composer can write it on paper and the singers can practice their parts separately, but harmony does not become real until the singers agree to follow the lead of the director, then open their mouths and sing together.

Unity and justice are two processes in a mutually reinforcing relationship; Bahá'u'lláh writes: "The purpose of justice is the appearance of unity among men."[11] Like unity, justice has a specific meaning to Bahá'ís. Justice is not an absolute, black-or-white standard. Instead, it is the consciousness of oneness of humanity expressed in action. Individually, most people have limited power to be either just or unjust. They can develop their own sense of what the oneness of humanity means, and treat others with fairness and equity, but when they come together in unity, as defined above, they receive the greater power to act with greater justice. When they do so, they create the conditions for greater unity. All that is necessary is to start the process.

Unity requires love at the level of the individual and justice at the level of society. Bahá'u'lláh has created a revolutionary system of institutions designed to meet the needs of a maturing humanity. Again from the House of Justice:

At the very core of the aims of the Faith are the establishment of justice and unity in the world, the removal of prejudice and enmity from among all people, the awakening of compassion and understanding in the hearts of men and women, and the raising of all souls to a new level of spirituality and behavior through the vitalizing influence of divine Revelation. The course set forth by Bahá'u'lláh for the attainment of these aims is the double task of simultaneously building an ideal society and perfecting the behavior of individuals. For this dual and reciprocal transformation He has not only revealed laws, principles and truths attuned to the needs of this age, but has established the very nucleus and pattern of those institutions which are to evolve into the structure of the divinely purposed world society.[12]

This is the essence of the Bahá'í plan for creating unity, justice, and peace. The Bahá'ís must simultaneously perfect their own behavior (i.e., increase their love) in ways that will contribute to the betterment of the world, and be engaged in building a new, alternative, global society based on a new system of decision-making that can act with justice and reinforce the spiritual, physical, and organic unity of humanity. Each of the following chapters will focus on an aspect of these twin tasks. But it is important to grasp at the very start that these tasks are simultaneous and interdependent. Bahá'ís will delay their gift of unity if they concentrate *only* on perfecting their behavior or *only* on building Bahá'u'lláh's new society. An often-used Bahá'í metaphor is that of a bird, whose flight is possible only when both of its wings are equally developed. If love and justice are viewed as wings for humanity's flight, then each must be balanced in order for it to soar.

Unity does not mean uniformity. The advancement of civilization invariably leads to more personal freedom, not less. In the future that the Bahá'ís are striving to build, the peoples of the world will still have their unique histories, languages, traditions, cultures, patterns of thought and habit, and national allegiances. But on the personal level they will see themselves first as human beings, and on the collective level, as citizens of the world, in agreement on how to act with justice. 'Abdu'l-Bahá makes an analogy between the world's peoples and the limbs and organs of the body. They are all different, they have their own functions and strengths, but they must all be under the direction of one life force for the whole organism to grow and function. The watchword of Bahá'u'lláh's ideal society is unity in diversity.

4

A New Race of Men Will Arise

In the last chapter it was observed that the Bahá'í writings frequently use biological growth and development as a metaphor for spiritual development. In particular, the process of human maturation and the concept of "coming of age" is used repeatedly. According to the Bahá'í teachings, the present age is the time of the spiritual maturation of society. One way or another, the nations and peoples of the world will come to see themselves and others as members of a single human family where the well-being of one depends upon the well-being of all.

A New Level of Personal Maturity

Bahá'u'lláh places much of the responsibility for the state of the world on its civil and spiritual leaders, who have, by and large, refused to consider unity and justice as the solution to the world's problems. But He also places great responsibility on His followers, whom He instructs to perfect their behavior and build an ideal society as a model for humanity. He expects of them a level of spiritual maturity higher than anything the world has seen.

We say that a person is mature when he can effectively arrange his day-to-day activities. He manages his time and money and is a responsible and trustworthy child, parent, spouse, friend, employee, neighbor, and citizen. He has a realistic appraisal of his strengths and weaknesses. He makes reasonable plans for the future and takes systematic actions for their realization. He uses the resources of family, community, and society to solve many of his own difficulties. But most of all, he balances his own needs and wants with those of his fellows, and is willing to give up some autonomy to a system he believes is just. Maturity is revealed in the balance that is struck between personal freedom and collective well-being.

In a spiritual context, a mature person takes responsibility for his relationship with God. He knows what God expects of him, is accountable for his own spiritual growth and progress, and takes action to remedy his deficiencies and "fight his own spiritual battles." Most of all, he can participate with other spiritual people in a nurturing, loving, and just community that shares responsibility for the well-being of its members.

Bahá'u'lláh's book of laws, the Kitáb-i-Aqdas, is His vision of a mature, reverent, moral, and responsible people united in a just society. He uses this book, first, to set forth the basic principles and imperatives that must guide society into the future, and the Covenant and institutions it requires to act with unity and justice. Second, He gives detailed rules for selected aspects of life where spiritual maturity and unity lead to distinctive patterns of Bahá'í life, for instance the requirements of daily prayer and annual fasting,* the simple Bahá'í rites of marriage and burial, and the guidance for individuals on the wise use of their time, talents, and money.

---

* Most religions teach fasting as a means of developing detachment from the material world. Many early Christians fasted each Wednesday and Saturday; Muslims fast during their month of Ramadan. The Bahá'í period of fasting is from March 2 through March 20. No food or drink is consumed from sunrise to sunset for those nineteen days. Fasting is limited to adults and youth in good health. Like other Bahá'í practices, it is a private responsibility.

The Kitáb-i-Aqdas should not, as I understand it, be treated as a complete and final rulebook for Bahá'í society. Instead, it is a blueprint and a vision for a well-ordered, just, and united civilization. Even during His lifetime, Bahá'u'lláh wrote several documents supplementing its teachings, instructed 'Abdu'l-Bahá to interpret and expand its provisions after his death (which he did, especially in his Will and Testament). Bahá'u'lláh also provided for an institution, the Universal House of Justice, to apply its principles to other aspects of life. Thus Bahá'ís are responsible for taking this blueprint and, in keeping with the provisions of the Covenant, creating the ideal society the world needs. Many of the teachings and provisions of the Kitáb-i-Aqdas will be explored in chapters to come.*

The Kitáb-i-Aqdas sets a high bar for humanity's individual and collective behavior. Shoghi Effendi summarizes the moral standards that Bahá'u'lláh enshrined in this book and 'Abdu'l-Bahá exemplified in his life as, first, "a rectitude of conduct" in collective life and, second, "a chaste and holy life" as the standard for one's private life:

---

* In some ways, the Kitáb-i-Aqdas is like other great documents that combine law and vision. It is not a work that can be approached casually or without historical context. Many of its provisions cannot be appreciated without some background in Islamic law as well the teachings of the Báb. And after its completion there are the authorized interpretations of 'Abdu'l-Bahá and Shoghi Effendi, followed by the analyses of its provisions by the Universal House of Justice. All of these are in a sense part of the text itself.

The English translation of the Kitáb-i-Aqdas contains significant supplementary material. In addition, there are two books which I have found helpful: Suheil Bushrui, *The Style of the Kitáb-i-Aqdas* (Bethesda, MD: University Press of Maryland, 1995) and Baharieh Rouhani Ma'ani and Sovaida Ewing, *The Laws of the Kitáb-i-Aqdas* (Oxford: George Ronald, 2004). I humbly suggest that anyone wishing to rigorously study the Kitáb-i-Aqdas acquire a good study guide and approach it not just as a book, but as a living document.

This rectitude of conduct, with its implications of justice, equity, truthfulness, honesty, fair-mindedness, re-
liability, and trustworthiness, must distinguish every
phase of the life of the Bahá'í community. . . .

[A] chaste and holy life, with its implications of mod-
esty, purity, temperance, decency, and clean-mindedness,
involves no less than the exercise of moderation in all that
pertains to dress, language, amusements, and all artistic
and literary avocations. It demands daily vigilance in the
control of one's carnal desires and corrupt inclinations. It
calls for the abandonment of a frivolous conduct, with its
excessive attachment to trivial and often misdirected plea-
sures. It requires total abstinence from all alcoholic drinks,
from opium, and from similar habit-forming drugs. It con-
demns the prostitution of art and of literature, the practices of nudism and of companionate marriage, infidelity
in marital relationships, and all manner of promiscuity,
of easy familiarity, and of sexual vices.[1]

This passage may bring to mind St. Paul's letters to the early
churches; the Bahá'ís share these same high moral standards
with the followers of many other faiths.

New Spiritual Capacities

But because this is the time of humanity's coming of age,
even rectitude of conduct and chaste and holy lives are not
sufficient. Bahá'u'lláh writes that "transformation in the
whole character of mankind" has always been God's motive in sending His divine teachers: "Is not the object of
every Revelation to effect a transformation in the whole

character of mankind, a transformation that shall manifest itself both outwardly and inwardly, that shall affect both its inner life and external conditions? For if the character of mankind be not changed, the futility of God's universal Manifestations would be apparent."[2]

Perfecting their behavior is just one of the twin tasks Bahá'u'lláh assigns to His followers. For the other, building a new society, Bahá'ís must adopt completely new behaviors and acquire new abilities. The moral qualities and virtues valued by all religions, starting with the love of God and reliance on Him, service to one's fellow man, trustworthiness, generosity, and fear of God's ultimate justice, are supplemented in Bahá'u'lláh's teachings by new dimensions of spirituality that make possible true unity among men. His spiritually mature person of the future will be as different from the typical person of today as the mature adult is from the adolescent. This person will be so different that Bahá'u'lláh actually refers to His people of the future as "a new race of men."[3] 'Abdu'l-Bahá explains it this way:

That which was applicable to human needs during the early history of the race can neither meet nor satisfy the demands of this day, this period of newness and consummation. Humanity has emerged from its former state of limitation and preliminary training. Man must now become imbued with new virtues and powers, new moral standards, new capacities. New bounties, perfect bestowals, are awaiting and already descending upon him. The gifts and blessings of the period of youth, although timely and sufficient during the adolescence of mankind, are now incapable of meeting the requirements of its maturity.[4]

One of the most thought-provoking teachings of Bahá-
'u'lláh, already introduced in chapter 2, is that, whenever
God sends a Manifestation with a new message for humanity, the power of this revelation alters the spiritual reality
of all things, and infuses new potentials into all people.
According to Him, the death of Christ on the cross made
possible great advances in human wisdom, learning, art,
and earthly sovereignty:

> Know thou that when the Son of Man [Christ] yielded
> up His breath to God, the whole creation wept with a
> great weeping. By sacrificing Himself, however, a fresh
> capacity was infused into all created things. Its evidences,
> as witnessed in all the peoples of the earth, are now mani-
> fest before thee. The deepest wisdom which the sages have
> uttered, the profoundest learning which any mind hath
> unfolded, the arts which the ablest hands have produced,
> the influence exerted by the most potent of rulers, are but
> manifestations of the quickening power released by His
> transcendent, His all-pervasive, and resplendent Spirit.[5]

Those who really embraced Christ's message found themselves transformed to a new spiritual being; this is how I
understand His call to be "born again."

In this day, Bahá'u'lláh's revelation creates new dimensions of spiritual potential within the individual and the
world collectively. The magnitude of the spiritual revolution occurring is tremendous:

> I testify that no sooner had the First Word proceeded
> [i.e., when God's new revelation appeared], through the

potency of Thy will and purpose, out of His mouth, and the First Call gone forth from His lips than the whole creation was revolutionized, and all that are in the heavens and all that are on earth were stirred to the depths. Through that Word the realities of all created things were shaken, were divided, separated, scattered, combined and reunited, disclosing, in both the contingent world and the heavenly kingdom, entities of a new creation, and revealing, in the unseen realms, the signs and tokens of Thy unity and oneness.[6]

These new realities are not visible to the naked eye. In ages past the gift of discerning the signs and tokens of God's unity and oneness was limited to a few mystics, philosophers, poets and prophets. In this day, however, these signs and tokens are everywhere, and the capacity to see them is given to all.

To See With The Eye Of Oneness

Bahá'u'lláh refers to the capacity to see and respond to this unity as "the eye of oneness."* Like "coming of age," the "eye of oneness" seems to me to be a potent metaphor for what is one of Bahá'u'lláh's pivotal teachings. To move the world toward peace and justice, its peoples must learn to

---

* He writes, "The essence of all that We have revealed for thee is Justice, is for man to free himself from idle fancy and imitation, discern with the eye of oneness His [God's] glorious handiwork, and look into all things with a searching eye." (Bahá'u'lláh, *Tablets,* p. 156.) The last chapter defined justice as the recognition of the oneness of humanity put into action. This quotation is one of several places where Bahá'u'lláh makes the connection between the collective concept of justice and the mature individual's ability to clearly "see" and comprehend humanity as one people and the world as one homeland.

see the interconnectedness and fundamental unity of all things, material and spiritual. All men have this new potential, this eye of oneness, but they must open it and learn to use it. The duty of each Bahá'í is to develop his own eye of oneness, and to gently assist others to open theirs, by education, guidance, and example. Bahá'ís believe this new capacity opens the door to the reconciliation of longstanding ethnic, racial, religious, and national divisions, divisions that become more senseless yet more destructive with every generation. Bahá'u'lláh writes: "So powerful is the light of unity that it can illuminate the whole earth."[7] Justice is this unity expressed.

I believe the awakening of the eye of oneness in all of humanity is the meaning of the "new race of men," "coming of age," and "spiritual maturity." I believe the "new heaven and new earth" spoken of in the Old and New Testaments are these new realities and this gift of the eye of oneness; why else would heaven have to be changed if not to allow for new spiritual realities? That all people now have this gift of the eye of oneness is the fourth defining belief of the Bahá'ís. They do not see any insurmountable obstacles to unity.*

---

* I've labeled the teaching of new spiritual realities and gifts as thought-provoking. Here is another of the thoughts it provokes in me: Each of God's Manifestations is the bearer of a message focused on a certain theme. Moses taught obedience of the law of God; Christ taught love and forgiveness on earth as it is in heaven; Muhammad taught submission of the will to God. Bahá'u'lláh teaches the unity of God and the oneness of religion and humanity. With each of these messages comes a new capacity within man to manifest its reality in this world. But along with the capacity to rise to higher levels of obedience, love, submission to God, or unity, comes the potential to do just the opposite. The Bahá'í practices discussed in the next eleven chapters each have an opposing practice to which many seem to subscribe; the idea of unity itself seems to be opposed in the West by the worship of individuality. I will return to this topic in chapter 14.

The body requires the right combinations of nutrition, exercise, rest, and medical care to develop its potentials. The mind requires a stimulating environment, teaching, training, and testing to achieve its greatest powers. Similarly, the human spirit does not develop by neglect. It needs the love and nurturing of other souls, and the training and testing provided by God through His Manifestations. By experiencing the Word of God, regular prayer and meditation, and obedience to the laws of God, the soul is led to spiritual growth and maturity. Just as with the body and mind, spiritual capacity is not realized overnight. Nor will everyone develop at the same pace. Not everyone has the potential to become an Olympic athlete, a Nobel laureate, or a spiritual giant. That is not important. Bahá'u'lláh gives this reassuring analogy: "The whole duty of man in this Day is to attain that share of the flood of grace, which God poureth forth for him. Let none, therefore, consider the largeness or smallness of the receptacle. The portion of some might lie in the palm of a man's hand, the portion of others might fill a cup, and of others even a gallon-measure."[8] Becoming a member of Bahá'u'lláh's new race of men does not depend on one's worthiness or material capacity. That is nobody's concern. God's loving grace is being poured out for all; anyone can attain his portion if he just strives for it.

A person's physical health and mental abilities require attention at every age. For Bahá'ís, spiritual development is also a lifelong activity. Some of the spiritual practices of the Bahá'ís, such as communion with God in prayer and meditation, fasting, charity, and study of the sacred texts, are found in most of the world's religions. As practiced by Bahá'ís, these are primarily individual or private activities. But Bahá'u'lláh has given His followers a collective spiritual mission: to create a new global society founded on the oneness of all peoples. To accomplish this mission, He has added new spiritual requirements and expanded the usual understanding of spiritual practices to include everyday activities such as work, decision-making, and social and economic development. His vision of the spiritually mature society and its citizens is rich and complex.

When God, through his Manifestations, infuses new spiritual potentials into the world, He also provides the mechanisms through which these capacities can be developed. One of the greatest of these mechanisms, as later chapters will illustrate, is participation in the Bahá'í community, involvement in its programs and activities, service on its institutions and association with fellow Bahá'ís. The worldwide Bahá'í community is an environment where each individual's capacity for creating unity can be systematically, organically, yet lovingly nurtured and developed.

These first chapters have described four essential components of Bahá'í belief. In sum, Bahá'ís see their religion as the latest in a never-ending series of unfolding, progressive revelations of God's love and guidance to humankind. The divine teachers, the Manifestations of God, are perfect conduits for God's grace and teaching, each infusing new spiritual capacities into humanity and giving the teachings by which these capacities are realized. Bahá'u'lláh's mission is to bring about peace, justice, and well-being by creating true unity among peoples and a new global civilization reflecting this unity. To achieve this mission, God has not only renewed the eternal moral teachings of all religions, but has also given to all people, individually and collectively, the capacity for a new level of spiritual maturity, new practices designed to realize this potential, and a new Covenant that assures divine guidance into the future.

Several metaphors have been introduced to explain these beliefs: the Bahá'í Covenant as a divine irrigation system to supplement the guidance of the Holy Spirit; the Manifestations of God as mirrors perfectly reflecting God's love and guidance to humanity; the idea of progressive revelation as successive grades in a school, each building on the teaching in the earlier ones; this day in history as the coming of age of the man's collective life on earth; the eye of oneness as God's spiritual gift to humanity at this time; and a new race of men as the transformation that will happen when this gift is realized.

Bahá'u'lláh's intention is to spiritualize not only man, but society as well. He has greatly expanded the idea of spirituality to include much more of man's collective life. He has created a laboratory, the Bahá'í community, where the new human capacities for mature collective action can be nurtured, practiced, and refined as a gift to humanity. Each of the next eleven chapters will examine one of the practices or institutions that is distinctive to the Bahá'í community and the teachings on why it is important and how it is attained. Each of these practices has at its core the imperative to create and foster unity among people. Each requires that people develop new dimensions of their spiritual selves, further opening their eye of oneness and causing them to reach a new level of maturity. Each, if adopted by a significant number of people, has the potential to recreate the norms and institutions of present society and help build the new global civilization envisioned by Bahá'u'lláh, the Kingdom of God on earth.

5

Independent Investigation of Truth

The first distinctive Bahá'í practice is to encourage everyone to search for God. This search is not just the privilege of the specially trained, the unusually wise or spiritual. Bahá'u'lláh affirms that, while not everyone has the same capacity for spiritual understanding, God has given everyone the basic capacity to know and love Him: "Having created the world and all that liveth and moveth therein, He, through the direct operation of His unconstrained and sovereign Will, chose to confer upon man the unique distinction and capacity to know Him and to love Him—a capacity that must needs be regarded as the generating impulse and the primary purpose underlying the whole of creation"[1]

The search for religious certitude is an intensely private and personal pursuit. It is impossible to give hard and fast rules or reasonable expectations. Everyone starts from a different place and proceeds along a different path. The important point is that this search is everyone's right (and indeed, responsibility), and for many people it becomes the grand adventure in their lives. What follows here is the Bahá'í perspective on the search for God and His Will.

Detachment is the Key

During His decade of exile in Baghdad, before Bahá'u'lláh announced to the followers of the Báb that He was indeed "Him whom God shall make manifest," He wrote three of

His best-known and best-loved works: the Kitáb-i-Íqán, the Seven Valleys, and the Hidden Words. None of these books deals directly with the specific new teachings He would later put forth. Instead, their focus is on the eternal question of religion: the relationship between God and His spiritual creation, man. The Seven Valleys is a mystical work that describes the journey of one who seeks God. To begin this journey is to enter "The Valley of Search," and the first steps are to free one's self from the limitations of past knowledge, and then to be patient:

> The stages that mark the wayfarer's journey from the abode of dust to the heavenly homeland are said to be seven. Some have called these Seven Valleys, and others, Seven Cities. And they say that until the wayfarer taketh leave of self, and traverseth these stages, he shall never reach to the ocean of nearness and union, nor drink of the peerless wine. The first is the Valley of Search. The steed of this Valley is patience; without patience the wayfarer on this journey will reach nowhere and attain no goal. Nor should he ever be downhearted; if he strive for a hundred thousand years and yet fail to behold the beauty of the Friend [God], he should not falter.[2]

Patience is not always regarded as a virtue in western society. There is no telling how long the search for God will take; it may be a hundred thousand years, or it may be completed, Bahá'u'lláh says, "in the twinkling of an eye."[3] The time it takes is irrelevant.

Bahá'u'lláh repeatedly identifies "blind imitation of the past" as one of the main obstacles to man's spiritual and social progress. In the next paragraph, He continues, "It is incumbent on these servants that they cleanse the heart—which is the wellspring of divine treasures—from every marking, and that they turn away from imitation, which is following the traces of their forefathers and sires, and shut the door of friendliness and enmity upon all the people of the earth."[4]

This is an interesting phrasing, to "shut the door of friendliness and enmity upon all the people of the earth." My understanding of this instruction is that one must be prepared to give up all attachments, including mortal love and hate, family and friends, if he is to be successful on this journey.* Readers who are comfortable with mystical writings will find in the Seven Valleys a seven-course spiritual feast. I regard this little book as, among other things, a manual on detachment.

The second of Bahá'u'lláh's books dealing with the search after spiritual truth is the Kitáb-i-Íqán. The purpose and tone of this book, as introduced in chapter 2, is more direct, dealing with the many obstacles that prevent

---

* In other writings, Bahá'u'lláh refers to the man-made universe of titles, distinctions, authorities, honors, and superstitions, to which people become attached, as the *Kingdom of Names*: "People for the most part delight in superstitions. They regard a single drop of the sea of delusion as preferable to an ocean of certitude. By holding fast unto names they deprive themselves of the inner reality and by clinging to vain imaginings they are kept back from the Dayspring of heavenly signs. God grant you may be graciously aided under all conditions to shatter the idols of superstition and to tear away the veils of the imaginations of men." (Bahá'u'lláh, *Tablets*, pp. 57–58.) Christ tells His disciples that, in order to enter the Kingdom of Heaven, they "must become as little children" (Matthew 18:1–4). I believe He was speaking of detachment from this man-made Kingdom of Names, and human imaginings of what God cannot do.

the seeker from realizing his goal. In the opening paragraphs of the Kitáb-i-Íqán, Bahá'u'lláh sets out the first steps by which a seeker can discover God. Again, detachment is the first step:

> No man shall attain the shores of the ocean of true understanding except he be detached from all that is in heaven and on earth. . . . The essence of these words is this: they that tread the path of faith, they that thirst for the wine of certitude, must cleanse themselves of all that is earthly—their ears from idle talk, their minds from vain imaginings, their hearts from worldly affections, their eyes from that which perisheth. They should put their trust in God, and, holding fast unto Him, follow in His way. Then will they be made worthy of the effulgent glories of the sun of divine knowledge and understanding, and become the recipients of a grace that is infinite and unseen, inasmuch as man can never hope to attain unto the knowledge of the All-Glorious, can never quaff from the stream of divine knowledge and wisdom, can never enter the abode of immortality, nor partake of the cup of divine nearness and favor, unless and until he ceases to regard the words and deeds of mortal men as a standard for the true understanding and recognition of God and His Prophets.[5]

Bahá'u'lláh, as discussed in chapter 2, holds religious leaders responsible for obstructing the search for God, because they have often used their positions of authority to hinder rather than encourage the exploration of religious truth.

He also presents the three proofs by which one can judge the truth of a religious claim. The strongest proof, the sacred texts of the religion, is a sign that everyone can evaluate.

Study the Words of the Manifestations

I am reluctant to give anyone else advice on how they should proceed on their search after certitude, but I believe the following four steps are in keeping with the spirit of Bahá'u'lláh's teachings: First, detach yourself from preconceived or traditional thoughts and worldly attachments. You must make up your mind to evaluate God's revelation on its own terms; this may not be as easy as it sounds. Second, read the sacred texts of the faith. If you are investigating the divine origins of the messages of Moses or Jesus or Muḥammad or Bahá'u'lláh, read Their words. Meditate on them and try to understand them to the best of your ability, a little at a time. Third, pray to God for guidance. Bahá'u'lláh says that our prayers will have an effect, even it we don't realize it at first. Step four is to be patient, very patient and very persistent, and return to step one.

If you are concerned foremost with investigating the station of Bahá'u'lláh and the truth of His message, and you are carrying on this search in private, do not limit yourself to information *about* the Bahá'í religion (like this book). Instead go to the source: the writings of Bahá'u'lláh and 'Abdu'l-Bahá. I suggest the Hidden Words of Bahá'u'lláh is a good place to start. Like in the Old Testament Book of Psalms and Christ's Sermon on the Mount, in the Hidden Words you will find the eternal religion of

God, "clothed in the garment of brevity." Read and meditate on each passage and judge its truth with your spiritual
compass. Try to look at all things with the eye of oneness.
If you are a Christian, ask Christ to guide you. If you find
the Hidden Words too abstract, try the *Promulgation of
Universal Peace,* which collects translations of talks given by
'Abdu'l-Bahá in America in 1911–12. On the other hand, if
you would rather join a group of other searchers, look for a
Bahá'í devotional gathering or study circle in your locality
(see chapter 15). The study circle format, with its structure
and trained facilitator, combined with the warmth and
adaptability of a small group, make it a comfortable place
to systematically explore the meaning and richness of the
Bahá'í sacred writings.

For a Bahá'í, the independent investigation of religious
truth is a spiritual practice that continues long after his formal enrollment in the Bahá'í community. It creates an atmosphere of openness and freedom both inside the community
and in their relations with others. Bahá'ís are encouraged to
ask questions about their religion, and they invite questions
from others. Since the Bahá'í Faith has no clergy (see chapter
6), and since no individual can claim an authoritative understanding of the Bahá'í teachings, answers to difficult questions can only come from the one authoritative source, the
sacred writings of the Faith. Every Bahá'í is encouraged to
study these writings to answer his own questions and those
of his fellow believers and friends, but no one has the right to
insist that his understanding is complete or correct. The translated writings of Bahá'u'lláh, combined with the authoritative interpretations given by 'Abdu'l-Bahá, the detailed expo-

sitions of Shoghi Effendi, and the letters of the House of Justice, together form a large and rich storehouse of guidance for Bahá'í individuals and communities.

Search Must be Followed by Action

If one's search for God is fruitful, and she acknowledges the signs of God's reality revealed in the teachings of a faith, the mature soul will naturally try to conform her actions to God's teachings. What is the point of seeking the most expert physician then ignoring his advice? Bahá'u'lláh writes, "The first and foremost duty prescribed unto men, next to the recognition of Him Who is the Eternal Truth [God revealed through the Manifestation], is the duty of steadfastness in His Cause."[6] For Bahá'ís, this means perfecting one's own behavior and joining with others in the building of a new civilization based on Bahá'u'lláh's standards, methods, and institutions. To withhold one's self from this process, no matter what the excuse, does not benefit anyone. In my understanding, God has given us the capacity for spiritual maturity in this day so that we might use it to be firm in the Covenant, and the Covenant so that we may unite with others to build a better world for all.

This first of Bahá'u'lláh's prescriptions, to encourage everyone to search for the truth of God and His will, is intended for everyone, whether they are His followers or not. All of humanity has been infused with the capacity for a new level of maturity, trustworthiness, and unified action. God trusts us all to use our spirits and minds for "the betterment of the world."

The Pursuit of Knowledge

The Bahá'í principle of unfettered search after truth applies also in more practical realms, such as human relationships. 'Abdu'l-Bahá says that many of the world's ills are based on mindless imitation of past behaviors:

God has not intended man to blindly imitate his fathers and ancestors. He has endowed him with mind or the faculty of reasoning by the exercise of which he is to investigate and discover the truth; and that which he finds real and true, he must accept. He must not be an imitator or blind follower of any soul. He must not rely implicitly upon the opinion of any man without investigation; nay, each soul must seek intelligently and independently, arriving at a real conclusion and bound only by that reality. The greatest cause of bereavement and disheartening in the world of humanity is ignorance based upon blind imitation. It is due to this that wars and battles prevail; from this cause hatred and animosity arise continually among mankind.[7]

Bahá'ís are expected to associate with the members of other religious communities. Since they accept the divine origin of all the world's major religions, they are free to read and study their sacred texts, to use them in their devotions and to defend their value.

Investigation of truth is not limited to spiritual and moral matters. Bahá'u'lláh encourages His followers to pursue all branches of learning, including the useful sciences and arts:

"It is permissible to study sciences and arts, but such sciences as are useful and would redound to the progress and advancement of the people. Thus hath it been decreed by Him Who is the Ordainer, the All-Wise."[8]

'Abdu'l-Bahá states that man's intellectual capacity, which makes science possible, is a divine gift:

Science is the first emanation from God toward man. All created beings embody the potentiality of material perfection, but the power of intellectual investigation and scientific acquisition is a higher virtue specialized to man alone. Other beings and organisms are deprived of this potentiality and attainment. God has created or deposited this love of reality in man. The development and progress of a nation is according to the measure and degree of that nation's scientific attainments. Through this means, its greatness is continually increased and day by day the welfare and prosperity of its people are assured.[9]

Again:

All blessings are divine in origin, but none can be compared with this power of intellectual investigation and research, which is an eternal gift producing fruits of unending delight. Man is ever partaking of these fruits. All other blessings are temporary; this is an everlasting possession. Even sovereignty has its limitations and overthrow; this is a kingship and dominion which none may usurp or destroy. Briefly, it is an eternal blessing and divine bestowal, the supreme gift of God to man. Therefore, you should put forward your most earnest efforts toward the acquisition of science and arts.[10]

Bahá'ís believe that man's spiritual capacity has increased with the coming of Bahá'u'lláh. This capacity is reflected in the increased pace of intellectual and especially scientific progress: "Now the new age is here and creation is reborn. Humanity hath taken on new life. The autumn hath gone by, and the reviving spring is here. All things are now made new. Arts and industries have been reborn, there are new discoveries in science, and there are new inventions; even the details of human affairs, such as dress and personal effects—even weapons—all these have likewise been renewed. The laws and procedures of every government have been revised. Renewal is the order of the day."[11]

There is some guidance in the Bahá'í writings about areas of intellectual endeavor that are not to be pursued. Bahá'u'lláh sets a standard that knowledge should lead to some benefit to humanity: "The Great Being saith: The learned of the day must direct the people to acquire those branches of knowledge which are of use, that both the learned themselves and the generality of mankind may derive benefits therefrom. Such academic pursuits as begin and end in words alone have never been and will never be of any worth."[12]

'Abdu'l-Bahá specifically mentions the "science of war" as something that should be dismissed: "In this most radiant century it has become necessary to divert these energies and utilize them in other directions, to seek the new path of fellowship and unity, to unlearn the science of war and devote supreme human forces to the blessed arts of peace."[13]

Science and religion are not independent branches of human pursuit. Each must serve as a check on the other. Religious principle steers people to sciences that provide benefit to humanity. Science helps weed out superstition from true religion: "Religion and Science are inter-twined with each other and cannot be separated. These are the two wings with which humanity must fly. One wing is not enough. Every religion which does not concern itself with Science is mere tradition, and that is not the essential. Therefore science, education and civilization are most important necessities for the full religious life."[14]

The Imperative of Education

Investigation of truth, whether spiritual or scientific, cannot happen in a vacuum. Education is essential to allow its pursuit. Another of the basic teachings of Bahá'u'lláh is the need for universal education of children. The Bahá'í religion, it should be clear by now, is scripture-based. Bahá'ís believe that the words of the Manifestations are endowed with a remarkable transformative power, capable of "converting satanic strength into heavenly power."[15] To take full advantage of this potency, the individual must be able to read and comprehend at a high level.

The Bahá'í view of education is not simply filling an empty vessel with knowledge. Instead, it is releasing the potentials placed by God within each person. Bahá'u'lláh writes, "Man is the supreme Talisman. Lack of a proper education hath, however, deprived him of that which he doth inherently possess. . . . The Great Being saith: Regard

man as a mine rich in gems of inestimable value. Education can, alone, cause it to reveal its treasures, and enable
mankind to benefit therefrom."[16] God has filled all with
potentials for good and beauty. True education assists the
individual in finding and developing his capacities.

There are many clear statements in the Bahá'í writings
about the importance of education and how it should be
provided for. According to Bahá'u'lláh, the education of
children is primarily the responsibility of the parents (and
in particular the father), but the rest of the community is
responsible for the education of children whose parents are
not able to provide for it: "Everyone, whether man or
woman, should hand over to a trusted person a portion of
what he or she earneth through trade, agriculture or other
occupation, for the training and education of children, to
be spent for this purpose with the knowledge of the Trust-
ees of the House of Justice."[17]

'Abdu'l-Bahá writes that the education of daughters is
more beneficial to the world than the education of sons:
"The girl's education is of more importance today than the
boy's, for she is the mother of the future race. It is the duty
of all to look after the children. Those without children
should, if possible, make themselves responsible for the
education of a child."[18] The importance and centrality of
education in the Bahá'í teachings will arise several more
times in chapters to come.

Sometimes when a Bahá'í gives a presentation on the
basic beliefs of his religion, he lists ten or eleven teachings
or "principles." Independent investigation of truth is usually first on the list. It is a reflection of a fundamental teach-

ing of his faith: In this day the spiritual realities of all things have changed. There are new insights to discover that were not possible a few generations ago, and new sciences to explore in the physical world. Man has changed too; he has a new capacity for spiritual maturity, both collectively and personally. This capacity translates directly into personal and collective responsibility for moral and material education, for spiritual growth and development. As he develops this capacity and opens his eye of oneness, he gradually becomes a member of a new race of men.

6

People Can Govern Themselves

The Bahá'í Faith is one of a few religions without a clergy. If you ask a Bahá'í why there is no clergy, you might not get a quick response. There seems to be little in the Bahá'í sacred writings addressing the question when phrased this way. The answer you will most often hear is that a clergy is simply not needed, or that Bahá'u'lláh made no provision for one. There is nothing in the Bahá'í practice that could be called a sacrament or ritual. Devotional services are comprised simply of readings and prayers from the sacred texts of the world's faiths along with music and art. The few rites, such as marriage and burial, are very simple and do not require a specially trained person. Most important, in this day of maturity, the responsibility for the basic, daily relationship between God and man rests on the individual.

No Need for Clergy or Ritual

Bahá'ís believe they are ultimately accountable to God for their own spiritual well-being. They are expected, in their private lives, to engage in the practices of daily prayer and meditation, systematic study of the Bahá'í and other sacred scriptures, and partake of the annual period of fasting. None of these practices requires an intermediary between the individual and his Creator. They are also expected to participate in their local Bahá'í communities. Once again, Bahá'u'lláh places His followers on a path toward spiritual maturity.

One particular religious practice that He expressly forbids is confession: "To none is it permitted to seek absolution from another soul; let repentance be between yourselves and God. He, verily, is the Pardoner, the Bounteous, the Gracious, the One Who absolveth the repentant."[1]

And in another document, He writes, "Such confession before people results in one's humiliation and abasement."[2] It is not God's desire that anyone be abased before another, and doing so does not lead to the kind of maturity that Bahá'u'lláh wishes for His followers.*

Besides personal prayer, study, and fasting, Bahá'ís as individuals are also responsible for introducing the beliefs and teachings of their religion to their relatives, friends, and neighbors, as their situations permit. This activity is called *teaching the Faith*.† Some take on more audacious teaching enterprises; one of the most audacious is to become what Bahá'ís call a *pioneer*, someone who leaves his native country to take up residence where there are few Bahá'ís. Unlike a missionary, no special clerical training is required to be a Bahá'í pioneer; neither are they accorded any special privileges in the community where they settle. Pioneering and other forms of Bahá'í service will be discussed in chapter 11.

---

*On the other hand, to ask for forgiveness from someone you wrong is a mark of maturity, and to seek help from a professional counselor is often wise and completely within the spirit of the Bahá'í teachings.

† I believe that teaching the Faith involves more than just Bahá'ís presenting the nuts and bolts of their religion to others. At least as important is the quest to assist others to develop their own spiritual selves and to "discern with the eye of oneness" God's handiwork.

The Two Arms of the Bahá'í Administrative Order

Though a Bahá'í might hesitate when asked about the lack of clergy, if you ask him how his religion is administered you should expect a lengthy response. The *Bahá'í administrative order*, as it is called, is well developed in the Bahá'í writings and is considered central to the goal of creating unity in the world. The administrative order, in some ways similar to that of other religions, divides the responsibilities between two branches, or as they are called, *arms*. The first arm is comprised of the elected decision-making institutions, the Local and National Spiritual Assemblies, Regional Councils, and the Universal House of Justice. Collectively, these are sometimes referred to as institutions of "the elected," or "the rulers." The second arm is comprised of the institutions of "the learned," at present consisting of the International Teaching Center, along with a worldwide body called the *Continental Boards of Counselors* and an *Auxiliary Board* which reports to the Counselors. In many areas, Auxiliary Board members appoint local assistants.

Bahá'u'lláh makes it clear that the learned among His followers have a very high station and great responsibility, yet one of the remarkable features of His administrative order is that the members of the institutions of the learned serve completely at the pleasure of the elected institutions. The learned have no decision-making responsibilities nor prerogatives except to advise and encourage individual Bahá'ís and their elected institutions, and to perform any duties assigned to them by these institutions. This may be the first time in religious history where authority for decision-making rests solely with people elected by and from the rank and file of believers.

The rest of this chapter will examine the workings of these two arms of the Bahá'í administrative order. Before starting on these details, however, it is most important to understand that Bahá'ís consider the administration of their religion as more than just a practical necessity. It is in reality a spiritual practice, like prayer and study. It is the nervous system of the new world society that they are beginning to build. They believe their spiritually based system of administration will eventually be a model for other societal institutions. This is the second distinctive practice of the Bahá'ís: With these simple institutions they can administer their Faith without the need for a traditional clergy, and even more, the principles under which these institutions operate will be a model for the institutions of a new global civilization.

The Nineteen Day Feast

The most basic Bahá'í administrative institution is the Nineteen Day Feast. The calendar established by the Báb and used by the Bahá'ís consists of nineteen months of nineteen days each. The first day of every month is a Feast day, which combines the devotional aspects of a worship service with community administration and fellowship. All Bahá'ís in a community, of all ages and histories, are members of this institution and are encouraged to participate in the Feast and bring matters for discussion. The purpose of the Bahá'í Feast is to create unity; in His book of laws, the Kitáb-i-Aqdas, Bahá'u'lláh states, "Verily, it is enjoined upon you to offer a feast, once in every month, though only water be served; for God hath purposed to bind hearts together, albeit through both earthly and heavenly means."[3]

Currently, in Bahá'í communities with ten or twenty or perhaps a hundred members, the Nineteen Day Feast is a comfortable gathering with plenty of time for discussion and fellowship. How it will scale up to meet the needs of communities with thousands, or tens of thousands of Bahá'ís, is something that is now being discussed and explored. None of the Bahá'í administrative institutions are fixed in form; all of them are expected to develop organically as the Faith grows.

The Local Spiritual Assembly

The most fundamental of the elected institutions is the Local Spiritual Assembly. As of 2003, there were approximately 11,000 Local Assemblies in the world, with some 1,200 in the United States. Bahá'u'lláh defines this institution in the Kitáb-i-Aqdas:

> The Lord hath ordained that in every city a House of Justice [Local Spiritual Assembly] be established wherein shall gather counselors to the number of Bahá [nine]. . . . It behooveth them to be the trusted ones of the Merciful among men and to regard themselves as the guardians appointed of God for all that dwell on earth. It is incumbent upon them to take counsel together and to have regard for the interests of the servants of God, for His sake, even as they regard their own interests, and to choose

that which is meet and seemly. Thus hath the Lord your God commanded you.*

'Abdu'l-Bahá, in his appointed role as interpreter of the writings of his father, has expanded on this brief description of the Spiritual Assembly, explaining the procedure for its election, its responsibilities, and methods of operation.

Some of the day-to-day responsibilities of the Local Spiritual Assembly are to promote the Bahá'í Faith in its locality, to see that Nineteen Day Feasts and Holy Days are observed and other important meetings are planned, to provide for the spiritual education of Bahá'í children and adults, and to administer membership roles, marriages, divorces, and funerals. Occasionally it must counsel individuals who are experiencing difficulties of various sorts and settle disputes and disagreements that might arise. It encourages local believers to participate in the local, national, and global plans of the Faith. The Spiritual Assembly is also responsible to be the voice of the Bahá'í Faith in the larger community. This often causes some initial confusion when

---

* Bahá'u'lláh, Kitáb-i-Aqdas, ¶30. 'Abdu'l-Bahá advises that, while the number of Bahá'ís is relatively small and their role in the larger community very limited, these institutions be referred to as *Spiritual Assemblies* rather than Houses of Justice. The writings of Shoghi Effendi, especially, emphasize the point that Spiritual Assemblies are now in the very early stages of their development, and more authority and responsibility will devolve to them as the Bahá'í religion grows. Although not presently referred to as Houses of Justice, it is interesting to note that in the quotation above, a connection is implied between the process of "taking counsel together" in the Spiritual Assembly meeting and seeking justice for the community. This topic will be taken up again in chapter 9.

some other institution wants to speak with the "leader of the Bahá'ís" and finds a group of nine, none of whom has the position of leader.

One of the most remarkable features of all the elected Bahá'í institutions, is that their members have no special power or authority outside of the meeting. Within the meeting, all nine members are equal. When the Assembly is not in session, the elected nine have no special status or prerogatives. Another distinguishing principle is that the members of the Spiritual Assembly regard themselves as responsible to God, not to the local community. This in itself creates a culture that fosters change, growth, and development instead of continually reinforcing the status quo. In a real sense, the institution is separate from its transitory membership.

The Bahá'í Electoral Process

The election of the Spiritual Assembly is by secret ballot, occurring annually at an administrative annual meeting held on April 21st, which coincides with the most important Bahá'í holy day, the Festival of Riḍván. Every adult believer is given the opportunity to vote for the members of the Spiritual Assembly in his locality, and is eligible to be elected as one of the nine members. There is no nominating or campaigning; in an atmosphere of prayer, voters simply write the names of the nine Bahá'ís they feel would be most suitable to the responsibilities of serving on the Spiritual Assembly for the coming year. The nine individuals with the most votes are elected.

The Bahá'í electoral process places a great deal of responsibility on the individual elector. To maturely exercise one's responsibility to vote, he must make the effort to become acquainted with as many Bahá'ís as possible in his locality, and must participate in the plans and activities of his Spiritual Assembly throughout the year so he will be able to assess the strengths and weaknesses of the current Assembly membership. The individual must also provide feedback to the Spiritual Assembly by participating in meetings such as the Nineteen Day Feast, where time is set aside to hear reports from the Assembly and issues are brought up for discussion.*

The Universal House of Justice emphasizes the unique, mature spiritual relationship that should exist between an Assembly and the electors:

> Equally significant to the procedures for election [of the membership of the Spiritual Assembly] . . . is the evocation of that rarefied atmosphere of prayer and reflection, that quiet dignity of the process, devoid of nominations and campaigning, in which the individual's freedom to choose is limited only by his own conscience, exercised in private in an attitude that invites communion with the Holy Spirit. In this sphere, the elector regards the outcome as an expression of the will of God, and those elected as being primarily responsible to that will, not to the constituency which elected them. An election thus

---

* Any concerns of a private nature should be taken to the Assembly in confidence.

conducted portrays an aspect of that organic unity of the inner and outer realities of human life which is necessary to the construction of a mature society in this new Age. In no other system do individuals exercise such a breadth of freedom in the electoral process.[4]

There is also a great deal of responsibility resting on the Spiritual Assembly to administer the affairs of the Bahá'í community, be its face to the rest of the world, and be responsive to the needs and concerns of individual Bahá'ís. Yet this responsibility rests on the institution. Any successes that are achieved as well as any failures that are endured are not the responsibility of individual Assembly members. Because Assemblies are not responsible to their electorates, it sometimes happens that unpopular decisions are made. One of the dimensions of Bahá'í spiritual maturity is evident when individuals support decisions and programs of their institutions even when their personal inclination might be to withhold it. Any decision of a Spiritual Assembly is eligible to be changed at some future time.

Service on a Spiritual Assembly can be a daunting task. If the activities of a community are complex, or there are many individuals appealing to the Assembly for advice and assistance, the hours can be long. As much work as practical is delegated to committees and task forces. At present only a few of the largest local Bahá'í communities in this country (the United States) pay one of their Assembly members (usually the secretary) as a part-time employee, but this number will no doubt increase as communities continue to grow. Shoghi Effendi has stated that the responsibilities of Assemblies will gradually increase, and the Bahá'ís will have to find creative ways to make this new system of religious administration practical while remaining true to its spiritual foundations as established in the sacred writings of the Faith.

Participation in the process of the Bahá'í administrative system is central to being a Bahá'í. To vote wisely, to give feedback, advice, and support, to serve if elected or appointed, and to wholeheartedly support its decisions, are really part of Bahá'u'lláh's Covenant with His followers. True unity, as discussed in chapter 3, requires a way to make decisions, and this is the Bahá'í way.

The National Spiritual Assembly

The institution of the National Spiritual Assembly is not established in the writings of Bahá'u'lláh but in the Will and Testament of 'Abdu'l-Bahá. It is elected and operates in a similar manner to the Local Assemblies. Once a year a local convention is held, to which all Bahá'ís are invited to attend. The adult Bahá'ís elect one or more delegates (proportional to the number of believers in the area). These delegates assemble later in the year in a national convention, hear the reports of the National Spiritual Assembly, vote for the nine members of the National Assembly for the coming year, and make recommendations for programs and activities. After the convention, they return to their home areas and present reports to the Bahá'ís in their localities. Every adult believer is eligible to be elected as a delegate to the national convention and as a member of the National Spiritual Assembly.

The Universal House of Justice

The members of the Universal House of Justice are elected every five years at an international convention. 'Abdu'l-Bahá specified its method of election, which is by vote of all members of National Assemblies. The responsibilities and operation of the House of Justice have been assembled and codified in a single document, published as *The Constitution of the Universal House of Justice*. The responsibilities of the House of Justice are drawn from the writings of Bahá'u'lláh, 'Abdu'l-Bahá, and Shoghi Effendi; essentially, they are to advance and protect the Bahá'í Faith and to safeguard the sacred texts on which it is based, to work for peace and unity among nations, and to promote the spiritual development of the individual Bahá'ís and the Faith's administrative order. In addition, it has the prerogative to enact laws on any matter not expressly recorded in the sacred texts, and to abrogate these at a later time. It is also the final arbiter of disputes and administers the activities of the Faith and stewards its material resources. As discussed in chapter 1, Bahá'u'lláh promises to guide its actions.

Any adult male Bahá'í in the world is eligible for election to the Universal House of Justice. The Kitáb-i-Aqdas refers to the members of the House of Justice as "men," and 'Abdu'l-Bahá confirms that, unlike Local and National Assemblies, membership on this body is limited to men, and that the reason for this will become clear at some future time. It sometimes causes confusion to have this one exception to the principle of the equality of women and men within the religion. Although Bahá'ís might be tempted to speculate on what the reason for this might be, it is at present unknown, and they have no alternative but to accept the statement as given. The Bahá'í writings state emphatically that there is no difference between women and men in their spiritual or mental capacity, so the reason must lie elsewhere. Members of the House of Justice, like members of Local and National Assemblies, have no special position or authority outside of their meeting.

The House of Justice and its supporting institutions, collectively known as the *Bahá'í World Center,* are located in Haifa, Israel, on the slope of Mount Carmel. These institutions include the International Bahá'í Archives, which houses the sacred texts and documents of the Faith, the Center for the Study of the Sacred Texts, which organizes, translates, and publishes these texts, and the International Teaching Center, which coordinates the work of the Continental Counselors (see below) and other activities such as social and economic development projects (see chapter 13).* Like the Local and National Spiritual Assemblies, the House of Justice is an institution of service not just to Bahá'ís but to the world.

An example of the continuing unfoldment of the Bahá'í administrative order, the institution of the Regional Bahá'í Council, was established in 1997 by the House of Justice in a handful of geographically large countries. The Regional Council is responsible for certain plans and activities best

---

* The resting places of the Báb, Bahá'u'lláh, 'Abdu'l-Bahá, and their families are also on Mount Carmel or nearby. These shrines and other historical sites are destinations of Bahá'í pilgrimage.

performed at a regional scale. Each is elected from among all the Bahá'ís in that region by the members of the region's Local Spiritual Assemblies.

The Bahá'í electoral process, with no nominations or campaigning and a pool of hundreds, thousands, or millions of candidates, is really a spiritual process emphasizing unity, maturity, and fairness. In order for the electors at any level to cast their ballots wisely, they must be acquainted with as many Bahá'ís as possible, either personally or through other channels. When the election is complete and the membership of the institution is announced, the elector may find few or none of his choices on the body. Yet he is expected to give his full support to the institution. When Bahá'í institutions at any level are guided by the principles of the teachings and have the unified support of the believers, they can wield great spiritual authority.

The Institutions of the Learned

The second arm of the Bahá'í administrative order are the institutions of the learned. During His lifetime, Bahá'u'lláh named four Bahá'ís of exceptional capacity and gave them the title of *Hands of the Cause of God.* They were charged with protecting and propagating the Faith. During his lifetime, 'Abdu'l-Bahá named four additional persons to this rank, and in his Will and Testament, in which he outlines much of the framework of the Bahá'í administrative order, he writes in detail about their appointment by the Guardian and their function to protect the Faith from division. Shoghi Effendi, during his years as Guardian of the Faith, appointed thirty-two men and women to the rank of Hand of the Cause, further clarified and organized their activities, and in 1954 created a secondary institution of the learned, the Auxiliary Boards, to assist the Hands of the Cause in their work. After Shoghi Effendi's unforeseen death in 1957, the Hands of the Cause collectively directed the affairs of the Faith until the first Universal House of Justice was elected in 1963.

Since the House of Justice does not have the authority to appoint Hands of the Cause, in 1968 it created a new institution, the Continental Boards of Counselors, which has gradually assumed the duties of the Hands of the Cause, including propagation of the Faith, and defending it from attacks from without and division from within. Separate Boards exist for five continental areas: Africa, the Americas, Asia, Australasia, and Europe. These Boards also appoint members to the Auxiliary Boards in their areas. Continental Counselors are appointed for five-year terms (they may be reappointed) and cannot simultaneously serve on any elected institution. There are 81 Counselors at present and about one thousand members of the Auxiliary Boards.

The rank of Continental Counselor is the highest position of individual authority in the Bahá'í Faith. No one would be considered for this position without an extended record of selfless Bahá'í service, knowledge, wisdom, and leadership. Yet their function is only to advise and inspire. These men and women perform no priestly duties, nor do they have the right to make administrative decisions or authoritative interpretations of Bahá'í scripture.

In summary, the Bahá'í Faith has no need for a traditional clergy. Bahá'ís are themselves responsible for their daily prayer, study of the sacred writings, the annual period of fasting, and teaching the Faith. The elected bodies of Local and National Spiritual Assemblies and the Universal House of Justice perform the administrative, decision-making requirements of the Faith, and the Continental Counselors and Auxiliary Boards serve in their roles to advise and encourage individuals and elected institutions.

Chapter 2 explained how true unity involves more than just good feelings among people; it also requires an agreed-to process for making decisions and taking action. The Bahá'í system of Spiritual Assemblies, each elected by a democratic process open to all, yet not responsible to the electors, is Bahá'u'lláh's system for making these decisions. Their decision-making process, called *consultation* (to be described in chapter 9), is designed to create unity and allow the Bahá'í community to move forward.

7

Elimination of All Prejudice

The teaching most universally associated with the Bahá'í religion is the imperative to eliminate all forms of prejudice. Bahá'ís the world over are associated with eliminating racism, class prejudice and extreme nationalism, emancipating women, and promoting the rights of children and all marginalized groups and minorities.

A New Spiritual Reality

The ethical teachings of Christ center on individual love, forgiveness, and humility: love your enemies and pray for them; forgive those who wrong you; do not judge; do not resist an evil person; be righteous but do not parade it before men; in all things rely first upon God. The Gospel records that "people were astonished at his doctine."[1] Is it any wonder? The teachings of the Manifestations have always been at variance with what we believe to be human nature; obedience to these commands is as challenging today as it was when Christ delivered them. Today Bahá'u'lláh reiterates all of Christ's admonitions, but then adds a new collective level of ethical responsibility. Not only are His followers to abide by these teachings as individuals, they are to consult and apply them as a unified community.

Many times in His writings, most notably in the Kitáb-i-Aqdas, Bahá'u'lláh calls on the Bahá'ís to "consort with the followers of all religions in a spirit of friendliness and fellowship." Then, in a later letter, He makes an audacious pronouncement that explains the spiritual underpinnings of this commandment. In my estimation, this single brief sentence encapsulates the spiritual basis of the social teachings of the Bahá'í Faith. It is worth reading several times, with an open mind (italics mine): "We have erewhile declared—and Our Word is the truth—: 'Consort with the followers of all religions in a spirit of friendliness and fellowship.' *Whatsoever hath led the children of men to shun one another, and hath caused dissensions and divisions amongst them, hath, through the revelation of these words, been nullified and abolished*."[2]

Here is my understanding of this pronouncement of Bahá'u'lláh: Whatever reasons I have for my prejudices, biases, and attitudes toward others, they are no longer valid. It doesn't matter what your ancestors did to my ancestors, or vice versa. It doesn't matter why differences arose in the past: gross injustices, wars, age-long struggles, even religious doctrines. It doesn't matter who started it. It doesn't matter what today's science or popular culture holds. It doesn't even matter what the scriptures of other religions say God desires. By these words God has now wiped the slate clean. Who was right and who was wrong is not important. This is the time to forgive the injustices of the past and begin to make new justice for the future. Separate but equal is not good enough either; you must treat everyone as your true brothers and sisters. All humanity is to be as one soul in one body.

Bahá'u'lláh is not asking His followers to root out their prejudices because that is the right thing to do (although it is). Nor is He saying this only for the benefit of the Bahá'ís. He is announcing a new spiritual reality. Everything that has divided us has been "nullified and abolished" by God's decree.

Statements such as this are stumbling blocks to many people. They cannot accept the possibility that God may make a distinction between one group of people and another, then a few thousand years later, unmake it, as if it had never been. But this is implicit in the idea of progressive revelation. With the coming of each of God's successive Manifestations, the spiritual world is made anew, and the social teachings of religion must now reflect this new reality. Bahá'ís believe that, with the coming of Bahá'u'lláh, all real barriers to the unification of humanity have been removed. What is left in the way are man's prejudices, traditions, and superstitions.

The quotation above refers specifically to prejudice based on religion. In other places, Bahá'u'lláh makes it clear that the basis for any and all prejudices have been removed by God's decree. Later in the same letter, nationalism is addressed. This passage is also worthy of careful reading: "The Tongue of Grandeur [God] hath, however, in the day of His manifestation proclaimed: 'It is not his to boast who loveth his country, but it is his who loveth the world.' Through the power released by these exalted words He hath lent a fresh impulse and set a new direction to the birds of men's hearts, and hath obliterated every trace of restriction and limitation from God's holy Book."*

---

* Bahá'u'lláh, *Tablets*, pp. 87–88. When I read these words, I imagine a quill pen in the hand of God, crossing out all the divisive language from the Bible, Koran, and other holy books, which people have magnified over the centuries. I don't believe this would take much ink.

Again, Bahá'u'lláh is announcing a new spiritual reality that "obliterat[es] every trace of restriction and limitation from God's holy Book," which requires a new commandment: "love the world."

Prejudice: The Root of Many Ills

Prejudice is the root cause of many of the world's stubborn problems. Referring to World War I 'Abdu'l-Bahá writes:

> Ye observe how the world is divided against itself, how many a land is red with blood and its very dust is caked with human gore. . . . And the breeding-ground of all these tragedies is prejudice: prejudice of race and nation, of religion, of political opinion; and the root cause of prejudice is blind imitation of the past—imitation in religion, in racial attitudes, in national bias, in politics. So long as this aping of the past persisteth, just so long will the foundations of the social order be blown to the four winds, just so long will humanity be continually exposed to direst peril.[3]

For many Bahá'ís, eliminating prejudice from their lives is a very difficult job. Prejudice is like an onion; you peel away one layer and you find another one, and you cry a lot in the process. Yet the mission of establishing the oneness of humanity requires this issue to be given preeminence. The Universal House of Justice instructs the Bahá'ís:

> Bahá'u'lláh tells us that prejudice in its various forms destroys the edifice of humanity. We are adjured by the

Divine Messenger [Bahá'u'lláh] to eliminate all forms of prejudice from our lives. Our outer lives must show forth our beliefs. The world must see that, regardless of each passing whim or current fashion of the generality of mankind, the Bahá'í lives his life according to the tenets of his Faith. We must not allow the fear of rejection by our friends and neighbors to deter us from our goal: to live the Bahá'í life. Let us strive to blot out from our lives every last trace of prejudice—racial, religious, political, economic, national, tribal, class, cultural, and that which is based on differences of education or age. We shall be distinguished from our non-Bahá'í associates if our lives are adorned with this principle.[4]

How to Blot Out Prejudice

The quest to "blot out from our lives every last trace of prejudice" is the third distinctive practice of the Bahá'í religion. How are Bahá'ís taught to approach this imperative? First of all, they recognize that elimination of prejudice is not optional. God commands all Bahá'ís to keep it in their thoughts "at all times." Another powerful pronouncement by Bahá'u'lláh should act as a wake-up call. It also deserves careful study:

O Children of Men! Know ye not why We created you all from the same dust? That no one should exalt himself over the other. Ponder at all times in your hearts how ye were created. Since We have created you all from one same substance it is incumbent on you to be even as one soul, to walk with the same feet, eat with the same mouth and dwell in the same land, that from your inmost being, by your deeds and actions, the signs of oneness and the essence of detachment may be made manifest. Such is My counsel to you, O concourse of light! Heed ye this counsel that ye may obtain the fruit of holiness from the tree of wondrous glory.[5]

Elimination of prejudice is, in the Bahá'í view, primarily a spiritual battle. The second thing that Bahá'ís do to wage this battle is to pray. Bahá'ís believe that prayer is a real tool that can change the hearts, not only of the supplicant, but of the world as a whole. There are many powerful prayers written by Bahá'u'lláh and 'Abdu'l-Bahá whose purpose is bringing people together in unity. Here is a prayer from 'Abdu'l-Bahá:

O Thou kind Lord! Thou hast created all humanity from the same stock. Thou hast decreed that all shall belong to the same household. In Thy Holy Presence they are all Thy servants, and all mankind are sheltered beneath Thy Tabernacle; all have gathered together at Thy Table of Bounty; all are illumined through the light of Thy Providence.

O God! Thou art kind to all, Thou hast provided for all, dost shelter all, conferrest life upon all. Thou hast endowed each and all with talents and faculties, and all are submerged in the Ocean of Thy Mercy.

O Thou kind Lord! Unite all. Let the religions agree and make the nations one, so that they may see each other as one family and the whole earth as one home. May they all live together in perfect harmony.

O God! Raise aloft the banner of the oneness of mankind.

O God! Establish the Most Great Peace.

Cement Thou, O God, the hearts together.

O Thou kind Father, God! Gladden our hearts through the fragrance of Thy love. Brighten our eyes through the Light of Thy Guidance. Delight our ears with the melody of Thy Word, and shelter us all in the Stronghold of Thy Providence.

Thou art the Mighty and Powerful, Thou art the Forgiving and Thou art the One Who overlooketh the shortcomings of all mankind.[6]

Prejudice is often the result of ignorance. In the absence of knowledge, the void is filled with imitation of the past. The third remedy is education; it is a powerful antidote to many ills. Today science has caught up to the Bahá'í teachings and rejects the idea of separate races; there is only one race of man, the human race. It is important that Bahá'ís understand this truth and teach it to others and to their children. Children's classes, which are taught in Bahá'í communities throughout the world, have the elimination of prejudice and the creation of unity among their primary objectives.

The fourth remedy to prejudice is obvious. 'Abdu'l-Bahá makes it crystal clear how Bahá'ís should behave toward people different from themselves: "The diversity in the human family should be the cause of love and harmony, as it is in music where many different notes blend together in the making of a perfect chord. If you meet those of different race and color from yourself, do not mistrust them and withdraw yourself into your shell of conventionality, but rather be glad and show them kindness. Think of them as different colored roses growing in the beautiful garden of humanity, and rejoice to be among them."[7] He instructs the Bahá'ís to step outside their comfort zones and associate with people others may find "undesirable." The benefits to the world outweigh the risks to the individual:

When a man turns his face to God he finds sunshine everywhere. All men are his brothers. Let not conventionality cause you to seem cold and unsympathetic when you meet strange people from other countries. Do not look at them as though you suspected them of being evil-doers, thieves and boors. You think it necessary to be very careful, not to expose yourselves to the risk of making acquaintance with such, possibly, undesirable people.

I ask you not to think only of yourselves. Be kind to the strangers, whether they come from Turkey, Japan, Persia, Russia, China or any other country in the world.

Help to make them feel at home; find out where they are staying, ask if you may render them any service; try to make their lives a little happier.

In this way, even if, sometimes, what you at first suspected should be true, still go out of your way to be kind to them—this kindness will help them to become better.

After all, why should any foreign people be treated as strangers?

Let those who meet you know, without your proclaiming the fact, that you are indeed a Bahá'í.

Put into practice the Teaching of Bahá'u'lláh, that of kindness to all nations. Do not be content with showing friendship in words alone, let your heart burn with loving kindness for all who may cross your path.[8]

The fifth way to blot out prejudice in oneself is to participate in the Bahá'í community. In many places, the local Bahá'í community is composed of people from a wide cross section of racial and ethnic groups, economic classes, ages, and educational backgrounds.* All the believers, each to the best of his ability, is striving to come to grips with and eliminate prejudice from their lives. This makes the Bahá'í community, in most places, a safe environment for people to associate with those different from themselves and practice God's commands.

America's Burden of Racial Prejudice

The building of communities free from prejudice has been, and continues to be, hard work. Each part of the world has its deeply ingrained patterns of thought and behavior. Every national community experiences some degree of inequality between women and men and prejudice based on religious heritage, national origin, or socioeconomic class. The United States has all of these, but its most virulent prejudice is that

---

* If your local community is not diverse, it will be someday soon. If it is diverse, it will become more diverse.

of race. Despite great strides towards its mollification, racial inequality and division remains, 140 years after the Civil War, a great, self-inflicted national wound. The elimination of racial prejudice, especially between the white and black "races," has been a central and ongoing concern of the Bahá'í community of the United States since its inception over one hundred years ago.

During his ministry, 'Abdu'l-Bahá was continually occupied with moving the white and black Bahá'ís of America toward true unity. At the beginning of the last century, due to the lack of easy communication between his home in the Middle East and America, most American Bahá'ís had only a rudimentary understanding of many of the fundamental teachings of their Faith. 'Abdu'l-Bahá was keenly interested to ascertain, from correspondents and visitors to Acre, the state of the relations between black and white Bahá'ís in America. He called for the integration of Bahá'í communities in the Southern states at a time when racial mixing was difficult and unpopular. He encouraged Bahá'ís to work for racial tolerance and understanding throughout the country by organizing "Race Amity" meetings and conferences. During his seven-month visit to this country in 1911–12, he demonstrated by word and deed that God considered white and black people equal in every regard, and that separation of the races was unacceptable. He advocated interracial marriage at a time when it was considered unwise by most people and was illegal in most states. 'Abdu'l-Bahá set a strong, unequivocal example of how Bahá'ís should behave to those of other races.

The example and teachings of 'Abdu'l-Bahá went beyond advocacy of equality between the races. They also called for what is now referred to as affirmative action, opening wide the doors to people who have traditionally been excluded. During his visit to America, 'Abdu'l-Bahá on many occasions proclaimed that people of African descent had a great spiritual capacity and destiny. Quoting his father, he several times compared them to "the pupil of the eye": "In this black pupil is seen the reflection of that which is before it, and through it the light of the spirit shineth forth."[9] One specific way in which 'Abdu'l-Bahá encouraged people of color was by establishing a rule that, in the election for the Local Spiritual Assembly, if there is a tie for the ninth position on the Assembly, and one of the persons is a member of a minority group, that person is automatically elected. Otherwise, a vote is taken between the tied candidates.

Shoghi Effendi followed on the path set by his grandfather and continued to urge the American Bahá'ís to root out racial prejudice from their lives and communities. In many letters, and especially in *The Advent of Divine Justice,* he called racial prejudice "the most vital and challenging issue facing the American Bahá'í community" and dealt extensively with how Bahá'ís, both white and black, should be attacking it. A detailed analysis of this letter is beyond the scope of this chapter, but *The Advent of Divine Justice* should be high on every American Bahá'í's required study list. Here is most of the first paragraph on racial prejudice, which gives an indication of the seriousness Shoghi Effendi attached to the issue:

As to racial prejudice, the corrosion of which, for well-nigh a century, has bitten into the fiber, and attacked the whole social structure of American society, it should be regarded as constituting the most vital and challenging issue confronting the Bahá'í community at the present stage of its evolution. The ceaseless exertions which this issue of paramount importance calls for, the sacrifices it must impose, the care and vigilance it demands, the moral courage and fortitude it requires, the tact and sympathy it necessitates, invest this problem, which the American believers are still far from having satisfactorily resolved, with an urgency and importance that cannot be overestimated. White and Negro, high and low, young and old, whether newly converted to the Faith or not, all who stand identified with it must participate in, and lend their assistance, each according to his or her capacity, experience, and opportunities, to the common task of fulfilling the instructions, realizing the hopes, and following the example, of 'Abdu'l-Bahá. Whether colored or noncolored, neither race has the right, or can conscientiously claim, to be regarded as absolved from such an obligation, as having realized such hopes, or having faithfully followed such an example. A long and thorny road, beset with pitfalls, still remains untraveled, both by the white and the Negro exponents of the redeeming Faith of Bahá'u'lláh.[10]

A paragraph later, Shoghi Effendi reaffirms his grandfather's insistence that within the Bahá'í community, minorities be given every encouragement:

If any discrimination is at all to be tolerated, it should be a discrimination not against, but rather in favor of the minority, be it racial or otherwise. Unlike the nations and peoples of the earth . . . who either ignore, trample upon, or extirpate, the racial, religious, or political minorities within the sphere of their jurisdiction, every organized community enlisted under the banner of Bahá'u'lláh should feel it to be its first and inescapable obligation to nurture, encourage, and safeguard every minority belonging to any faith, race, class, or nation within it.[11]

But Bahá'u'lláh gives the community an ethical responsibility as well. Because of the unequal structural relationship between whites and blacks in America, the universal prescription of love and forgiveness must be applied unequally. White and black Bahá'ís have special responsibilities just because they are white or black. Shoghi Effendi says that white Bahá'ís must exhibit true, unconditional love toward their black brethren:

Let the white make a supreme effort in their resolve to contribute their share to the solution of this problem, to abandon once for all their usually inherent and at times subconscious sense of superiority, to correct their tendency towards revealing a patronizing attitude towards the members of the other race, to persuade them through their intimate, spontaneous and informal association with them of the genuineness of their friendship and the sincerity of their intentions, and to master their impatience of any lack of responsiveness on the part of a people who have received, for so long a period, such grievous and slow-healing wounds.[12]

At the same time, African-American Bahá'ís must be ready to respond with unconditional forgiveness for past injustices: "Let the Negroes, through a corresponding effort on their part, show by every means in their power the warmth of their response, their readiness to forget the past, and their ability to wipe out every trace of suspicion that may still linger in their hearts and minds."[13]

These are not easy prescriptions for either party to embrace. They require both extreme humility and courage on the personal level, faith that God has indeed made the roots of this division, as Bahá'u'lláh has proclaimed, nullified and abolished, and the knowledge that this is God's will. Shoghi Effendi continues, "Let neither think that the solution of so vast a problem is a matter that exclusively concerns the other. Let neither think that such a problem can either easily or immediately be resolved. . . . Let neither think that anything short of genuine love, extreme patience, true humility, consummate tact, sound initiative, mature wisdom, and deliberate, persistent, and prayerful effort, can succeed in blotting out the stain which this patent evil has left on the fair name of their common country."[14]

I believe this prescription of collective love and forgiveness, carefully and correctly applied, as Shoghi Effendi does in *The Advent of Divine Justice,* can be a model for the healing of many longstanding divisions that continue to threaten humanity's well-being.

The elimination of prejudice within the Bahá'í community must be accompanied by working for the same in the larger community and by calling for justice at the institutional level. Individual Bahá'ís have, for almost one hundred years, been at the forefront of programs to promote racial conciliation and unity. (One of these programs is discussed in chapter 13.) They have also, as their opportunities, means, and abilities have allowed, called and worked for justice in employment, education, housing, and social services.

As the Bahá'í community becomes larger and more mature, it is beginning to take its place in the world as a voice for true unity and the actions that are necessary to create it. In the past two decades, the work of individuals in the field of social justice has been reinforced by the work of the Bahá'í International Community and National Spiritual Assembly of the United States, which have prepared papers clearly enunciating the Bahá'í view that social progress rests on the elimination of prejudice in its many forms and the creation of the bonds of true unity among peoples. One of these papers is *The Vision of Race Unity,* released in 1991 by the U.S. National Spiritual Assembly. It catalogs the price this country pays for failing to solve the problem of racism: poverty, hopelessness, lack of education, and failure in world leadership. It calls for government to do its part to address these wrongs, but puts the onus of responsibility on the individual American:

Our appeal is addressed primarily to the individual American, because the transformation of a whole nation ultimately depends on the initiative and change of character of the individuals who compose it. No great idea or plan of action by the government or other interested organizations can hope to succeed if the individual neglects to respond in his or her own way as personal circumstances and opportunities permit. And so we respectfully and urgently call upon our fellow Americans of whatever background to look at the racial situation with new eyes and with a new determination to lend effective support to the resolution of a problem that hinders the advance of this great republic toward the full realization of its glorious destiny.[15]

The Equality of Women and Men

This discussion has focused on racial prejudice. The equality of women and men, which while not "the most challenging issue" in the United States, is still a formidable issue for Americans and the American Bahá'í community. The Bahá'í writings clearly state that, while women and men have some different functions in the family and society, there are no differences in the education they should receive, or the economic, legal, and social opportunities they should experience. In fact, just as in the case of racial prejudice, the inequality between men and women hurts both parties. The equal involvement of women is necessary for society to advance. One of 'Abdu'l-Bahá's best-known public talks uses the analogy of the two wings of a bird: "The world of humanity is possessed of two wings: the male and the female. So long as these two wings are not equivalent in strength, the bird will not fly. Until womankind reaches the same degree as man, until she enjoys the same arena of activity, extraordinary attainment for humanity will not be realized; humanity cannot wing its way to heights of real attainment. When the two wings or parts become equivalent in strength, enjoying the same prerogatives, the flight of man will be exceedingly lofty and extraordinary."[16]

In 1999, the U.S. National Spiritual Assembly issued an open letter entitled *Two Wings of a Bird: The Equality of Women and Men*. Like *The Vision of Race Unity*, it summarizes the Bahá'í teachings on this matter. It calls upon men to do their duty to work for the rights of women:

Men have an inescapable duty to promote the equality of women. The presumption of superiority by men thwarts the ambition of women and inhibits the creation of an environment in which equality may reign. The destructive effects of inequality prevent men from maturing and developing the qualities necessary to meet the challenges of the new millennium. *"As long as women are prevented from attaining their highest possibilities,"* the Bahá'í Writings state, *"so long will men be unable to achieve the greatness which might be theirs."* It is essential that men engage in a careful, deliberate examination of attitudes, feelings, and behavior deeply rooted in cultural habit, that block the equal participation of women and stifle the growth of men. The willingness of men to take responsibility for equality will create an optimum environment for progress: *"When men own the equality of women there will be no need for them to struggle for their rights!"* [17]

The creation of the bonds of love and justice among all people is the central mission of the Bahá'í Faith. The elimination of all forms of prejudice is one of the primary means for its achievement. Prejudices of one kind or another are deeply rooted within peoples and cultures. They did not arise overnight, nor will they be uprooted in a day or a generation. But Bahá'ís believe that God has "obliterated every trace of restriction and limitation from God's holy book" and "nullified and abolished" the reasons for the divisions of the past. They believe that God has given them the mission of making this new spiritual reality a material reality. Accomplishing this mission requires both faith and action; faith that God had indeed made the roots of prejudice irrelevant, then building a community where education and fellowship among people is supported and reinforced and where collective action can be taken with justice.

Bahá'u'lláh teaches that the reasons for divisions among people have been abolished by God's decree. The implications of this for the world are, I believe, only partly understood by His followers at this time. As the world becomes smaller, future generations will grapple anew with this decree and its ramifications. The onion has still more layers to peel.

8

Gossip Is the Greatest Vice

In keeping with the perspective that humankind is reaching a new stage of maturity, most of the Bahá'í teachings are expressed in positive fashion, what man *should* do, not as sins, what man should not. One important exception to this are Bahá'u'lláh's teachings on gossip and backbiting.

Gossip, Faultfinding, Slander, and Backbiting Condemned

One of the most remarkable teachings of Bahá'u'lláh, and in some ways the most sobering, designed to break down one of the great barriers to unity among people, is that gossip, fault-finding, slander, and backbiting are regarded as the greatest of human vices. This teaching is repeated many times in the writings of Bahá'u'lláh, 'Abdu'l-Bahá, and Shoghi Effendi. In the Kitáb-i-Aqdas, Bahá'u'lláh mentions slander and backbiting in the same sentence as murder and adultery: "Ye have been forbidden to commit murder or adultery, or to engage in backbiting or calumny; shun ye, then, what hath been prohibited in the holy Books and Tablets."* In the Kitáb-i-Íqán, He says

---

* Bahá'u'lláh, Kitáb-i-Aqdas, ¶19. The connection Bahá'u'lláh makes between backbiting and murder is not unique. The Manifestations of God continually emphasize the seriousness of spiritual, what some might call "mental," sins. Christ makes the almost the identical connection, saying that anger and name calling are as serious as murder: "You have heard that it was said to the people long ago, 'Do not murder, and anyone who murders will be

that backbiting will prevent the seeker from attaining to the knowledge of God, going so far as to say that it may extinguish one's soul: "That seeker should also regard backbiting as grievous error, and keep himself aloof from its dominion, inasmuch as backbiting quencheth the light of the heart, and extinguisheth the life of the soul."[1]

And in the Hidden Words Bahá'u'lláh gives gossip the strongest condemnation: O Son of Man! Breathe not the sins of others so long as thou art thyself a sinner. Shouldst thou transgress this command, accursed wouldst thou be, and to this I bear witness."[2]

'Abdu'l-Bahá calls backbiting the worst human quality and identifies it as a barrier to spiritual growth and happiness: "The worst human quality and the most great sin is backbiting, more especially when it emanates from the tongues of the believers of God. If some means were devised so that the doors of backbiting were shut eternally and each one of the believers unsealed his lips in praise of others, then the Teachings of His Holiness Bahá'u'lláh would spread, the hearts be illumined, the spirits glorified, and the human world would attain to everlasting felicity."[3]

Why this emphasis on eliminating fault-finding and backbiting? Shoghi Effendi explains that these vices prevent the unity among people that the Bahá'í Faith was created to promote:

---

subject to judgment.' But I tell you that anyone who is angry with his brother will be subject to judgment. Again, anyone who says to his brother, 'Raca,' [worthless] is answerable to the Sanhedrin. But anyone who says, 'You fool!' will be in danger of the fire of hell." (Matthew 5:21–2) It is clear that Christ was not mincing words when He speaks of the evils of anger and name calling, yet this teaching seems to have little impact today in Western society.

If we Bahá'ís cannot attain to cordial unity among ourselves, then we fail to realize the main purpose for which the Báb, Bahá'u'lláh and the Beloved Master ['Abdu'l-Bahá] lived and suffered.

In order to achieve this cordial unity one of the first essentials insisted on by Bahá'u'lláh and 'Abdu'l-Bahá is that we resist the natural tendency to let our attention dwell on the faults and failings of others rather than on our own. Each of us is responsible for one life only, and that is our own. . . . On no subject are the Bahá'í teachings more emphatic than on the necessity to abstain from faultfinding and backbiting while being ever eager to discover and root out our own faults and overcome our own failings.[4]

Gossip, slander, and backbiting are defined as discussing the faults of others in their absence. Criticizing people to their face, in any manner that might cause humiliation or offense, is also strongly condemned. 'Abdu'l-Bahá writes:

O army of God! Beware lest ye harm any soul, or make any heart to sorrow; lest ye wound any man with your words, be he known to you or a stranger, be he friend or foe. Pray ye for all; ask ye that all be blessed, all be forgiven. Beware, beware, lest any of you seek vengeance, even against one who is thirsting for your blood. Beware, beware, lest ye offend the feelings of another, even though he be an evil-doer, and he wish you ill. Look ye not upon the creatures, turn ye to their Creator. See ye not the never-yielding people, see but the Lord of Hosts. Gaze ye not down upon the dust, gaze upward at the shining sun, which hath caused every patch of darksome earth to glow with light.[5]

The Bahá'í teachings on faultfinding and backbiting cannot be regarded as a *new* practice. In the Gospel, Christ gives a very similar counsel: "Do not judge, or you too will be judged. . . .Why do you look at the speck of sawdust in your brother's eye and pay no attention to the plank in your own eye? How can you say to your brother, 'Let me take the speck out of your eye,' when all the time there is a plank in your own eye? You hypocrite, first take the plank out of your own eye, and then you will see clearly to remove the speck from your brother's eye."[6]

Yet today, in Western society, these clear teachings of Christ are ignored; nothing is so common as gossip, backbiting, name-calling, and hurtful criticism. Look at the home, the workplace, and in front of the television, where Americans spend their typical day. How many hours in the day are we subjected to, and do we participate in, these vices? It seems at times that backbiting, gossip, and criticism are the primary ways many people relate to their families, friends, and associates. The renewal of these teachings is imperative, or unity will be impossible.

Five Steps to Fight Gossip

The Bahá'í Faith teaches that not only are these vices a waste of time, they are detrimental to the spiritual health of everyone they touch. Even if one manages not to participate in these activities, the environment they create is like secondhand smoke to the spirit. How are Bahá'ís taught to respond to this polluted environment? There are several explicit teachings addressing different aspects of this problem. First, if someone observes a fault in another, the clear prescription is to conceal it, as God is concealing his own failings: "Blessed are the learned that pride not themselves on their attainments; and well is it with the righteous that mock not the sinful, but rather conceal their misdeeds, so that their own shortcomings may remain veiled to men's eyes."[7]

It is not enough to avoid gossip and backbiting; one must consciously try to do the opposite. The second instruction is that Bahá'ís are to continually support and encourage one another:

> The Cause of the Ancient Beauty [Bahá'u'lláh] is the very essence of love, the very channel of oneness, existing only that all may become the waves of one sea, and bright stars of the same endless sky, and pearls within the shell of singleness, and gleaming jewels quarried from the mines of unity; that they may become servants one to another, adore one another, bless one another, praise one another; that each one may loose his tongue and extol the rest without exception, each one voice his gratitude to all the rest; . . . that they should see nothing but good in one another, hear nothing but praise of one another, and speak no word of one another save only to praise.[8]

'Abdu'l-Bahá tells a story about Christ, who found beauty even in the most repulsive sight:

> One must see in every human being only that which is worthy of praise. When this is done, one can be a friend to the whole human race. If, however, we look at people from the standpoint of their faults, then being a friend to them is a formidable task.

123

It happened one day in the time of Christ—may the life of the world be a sacrifice unto Him—that He passed by the dead body of a dog, a carcass reeking, hideous, the limbs rotting away. One of those present said: 'How foul its stench!' And another said: 'How sickening! How loathsome!' To be brief, each one of them had something to add to the list.

But then Christ Himself spoke, and He told them: 'Look at that dog's teeth! How gleaming white!'

The Messiah's sin-covering gaze did not for a moment dwell upon the repulsiveness of that carrion. The one element of that dead dog's carcass which was not abomination was the teeth: and Jesus looked upon their brightness.

Thus is it incumbent upon us, when we direct our gaze toward other people, to see where they excel, not where they fail.[9]

Third, when tempted to look at the shortcomings of another, one must instead look at his own faults. This is the essence of Christ's teaching quoted above. There is a record of a conversation with 'Abdu'l-Bahá that took place in Paris in 1913, in which he was asked just this question: "He was asked, 'How shall I overcome seeing the faults of others—recognizing the wrong in others?', and He replied: 'I will tell you. Whenever you recognize the fault of another, think of yourself! What are my imperfections? and try to remove them. Do this whenever you are tried through the words or deeds of others. Thus you will grow, become more perfect. You will overcome self, you will not even have time to think of the faults of others.'"[10]

A fourth aspect of the problem of gossip and backbiting, is what to do when it enters a conversation. The Bahá'ís are instructed not just to ignore gossip, but to act to stop it: "It is obvious that if we listen to those who complain to us about the faults of others we are guilty of complicity in their backbiting. We should therefore, as tactfully as possible, but yet firmly, do our utmost to prevent others from making accusations or complaints against others in our presence."[11]

And the fifth teaching, a very difficult one, is that, if one is the target of gossip, backbiting, or hurtful criticism, the Bahá'í standard is to instantly forgive the perpetrator. 'Abdu'l-Bahá says,

> Recognize your enemies as friends, and consider those who wish you evil as the wishers of good. You must not see evil as evil and then compromise with your opinion, for to treat in a smooth, kindly way one whom you consider evil or an enemy is hypocrisy, and this is not worthy or allowable. You must consider your enemies as your friends, look upon your evil-wishers as your well-wishers and treat them accordingly. Act in such a way that your heart may be free from hatred. Let not your heart be offended with anyone. If some one commits an error and wrong toward you, you must instantly forgive him.[12]

Occasionally, a Bahá'í will become aware of an issue involving another person that is so serious that the well-being of other individuals, or of the Bahá'í community, is threatened. These sorts of matters should be brought to the attention of the Local Spiritual Assembly and left for it to deal with. It is the responsibility of this institution to protect the Bahá'í community from harm, while the individual Bahá'í is only responsible to love his fellow believers.*

Although the primary relationship among individuals should be love and forgiveness, the new society envisaged by Bahá'u'lláh requires more than love and forgiveness at the level of the individual. It also requires order and justice; the same people who are required to ignore the faults of others and instantly forgive their transgressions are expected to know right from wrong and, in the consultative group (the Spiritual Assembly or House of Justice), join their views and establish justice. To be able to perform both these roles is a sign of spiritual maturity and one of the hallmarks of Bahá'u'lláh's new race of men.

It is apparent by now that these teachings set a very high standard for interpersonal behavior within the Bahá'í community. Bahá'ís of all backgrounds are going to struggle to resist the urges to gossip, criticize, and faultfind. As hard as it is to keep one's mouth shut, it is more difficult yet to love and support people who are just as imperfect as you. And to instantly forgive, when you are the one hurt, may be the hardest teaching of all. These teachings are one of the major tests on the path to spiritual maturity.

---

* The reader may recall from chapter 5 that in the Kitáb-i-Aqdas Bahá'u'lláh required that Houses of Justice be established in every town, but that, at their current stage of development they are known as Spiritual Assemblies. In the future, when the number of Bahá'ís is much larger, the responsibilities of Spiritual Assemblies more complex and their level of wisdom greater, they will grow into the role of Houses of Justice. But even now, they are often called on to act, when the welfare of others is at stake, with justice.

Building a new, distinctive society is a difficult process. It does not happen overnight. There will be times in some Bahá'í communities when gossip and criticism end in division or disunity among the Bahá'ís. The progress of the Bahá'í Faith in that locality will be seriously affected for a while. One time this can happen is when the Faith is growing rapidly and the many new Bahá'ís have not yet grasped the importance of these teachings. It is the responsibility of the older and more senior Bahá'ís, as well as the Spiritual Assembly and the institutions of the learned, to help guide the community through these times. Spiritual education is also required, and Bahá'ís are now working hard to develop a systematic method of education and training to allow all believers, new and old, to understand the new imperatives revealed by Bahá'u'lláh. This will be the topic of chapter 15.

9

Decision-Making is a Spiritual Activity

In the history of the Bahá'í religion briefly summarized in chapter 1 it was explained that, since the death of Shoghi Effendi in 1957, there is no single leader of the Bahá'í Faith. At the worldwide level, the Universal House of Justice collectively fills the role of leader; at the national and local levels, there are Spiritual Assemblies and Regional Councils. Each of these bodies is elected according to the democratic and spiritual principles of the Faith. There are no individual leaders, parties, factions, constituencies, nominations, or platforms. Their deliberations use a method of group-based decision-making Bahá'ís call *consultation*.

Consultation: The Foundation of Collective Life

Bahá'u'lláh asks His followers to consult, calling it one of the paths to divine wisdom: "The Great Being saith: The heaven of divine wisdom is illumined with the two luminaries of consultation and compassion. Take ye counsel together in all matters, inasmuch as consultation is the lamp of guidance which leadeth the way, and is the bestower of understanding."[1]

In another place, Bahá'u'lláh makes it clear that consultation is the foundation of the collective life of the community: "In all things it is necessary to consult. This matter should be forcibly stressed by thee, so that consultation may be observed by all. The intent of what hath been revealed from the Pen of the Most High is that consultation may be fully carried out among the friends, inasmuch as it is and will always be a cause of awareness and of awakening and a source of good and well-being."[2]

The Bahá'í model of community life emphasizes collaboration, cooperation, consultation, and unity-building. 'Abdu'l-Bahá says that consultation multiplies the power of the individual: "The views of several individuals are assuredly preferable to one man, even as the power of a number of men is of course greater than the power of one man."[3]

This is not to diminish the importance of individual initiative. There is much work that can only be done by the individual, but the "solid foundation" of Bahá'í activity is the group, whether the family, the Nineteen Day Feast, the Local or National Spiritual Assembly, a committee or task force, or an informal group gathered to address a problem in their neighborhood.

The Method of Consultation

What exactly is consultation? It does not reduce to a simple formula, but some of its primary features are as follows. First, Bahá'ís consider consultation a spiritual practice. This means that it begins by people gathering with a spiritual attitude and seeing themselves as in the presence of God: "The first duty of the members is to effect their own unity and harmony, in order to obtain good results. If there be no unity, or the Committee becomes the cause of inharmony, undoubtedly, it is better that it does not exist. . . . Therefore, when the unity of the members of the Committee is established, their second duty is to read the verses and communes, to be in a state of commemoration and mindfulness, that they may see each other as if in the presence of God."[4]

The next step is to freely discuss the matter at hand. In consultation all are equal and no one's idea is set above the others. Once a thought or idea is voiced, it is no longer the "property" of the person who voiced it, but of the group. There is no place for partisanship, platforms, debate, propaganda, bullying, or an adversarial atmosphere. The ideas can be accepted, rejected, modified, or combined with other ideas, as the group desires.

> The second principle is that of detachment in consultation. The members of an Assembly must learn to express their views frankly, calmly, without passion or rancor. They must also learn to listen to the opinions of their fellow members without taking offense or belittling the views of another. Bahá'í consultation is not an easy process. It requires love, kindliness, moral courage and humility. Thus no member should ever allow himself to be prevented from expressing frankly his view because it may offend a fellow member; and realizing this, no member should take offense at another member's statements.[5]

The goal of consultation is unanimity. Usually there will be agreement on the course of action. But if, after all views are put forth and discussed there is no agreement, it is permissible to settle the issue by a vote, or to postpone the final decision to gather more information or to allow the participants time to reflect.

The final step in consultation, and perhaps the most remarkable, is that once a decision is reached, whether by consensus or vote, it becomes the decision of the group. The count of votes is never announced; there is never a dissenting or minority view. All members are expected to support the decision wholeheartedly. In the case of Spiritual Assemblies, the expectation of obedience extends to the entire community. If someone is convinced that the decision violates an explicit teaching of the Faith, she is free to appeal the matter to the next higher administrative institution, but in the mean time she is expected to abide by the current decision.

Consultation can be a long and delicate process. It requires capacities that are often latent and unappreciated in contemporary Western society. It has little to do with speed and efficiency, and much to do with inclusion, equality, and unity. In the case of a Spiritual Assembly or other Bahá'í institution there is usually a chairperson whose task it is to keep the consultation on topic and orderly, and to make sure no person dominates the discussion, but that the process belongs to the entire body.

Unity Behind the Decision is Imperative

What if a consultative body makes a decision that, in retrospect, is found to be incorrect? They correct it and move on. The mistake will be more apparent, and therefore easily corrected, if the community is united behind the decision. Unified action is a goal of consultation; 'Abdu'l-Bahá explains that it is much better to be united and wrong than to

be split into contending factions: "Though one of the parties may be in the right and they disagree that will be the
cause of a thousand wrongs, but if they agree and both
parties are in the wrong, as it is in unity the truth will be
revealed and the wrong made right."[6] And again:

> Blessed are they who are the means of making unity
> among the friends, and pity on those who *in the right or
> wrong* are the cause of discord. For instance: when one is
> in the right in a case in dispute, and his minority pre-
> vents him from establishing this rightful matter, instead
> of agitating the subject, if he will humbly submit to sac-
> rifice his position for the sake of unity and peace, God
> will accept that sacrifice and ere long the rightful matter
> will be established without any further dispute, by the
> Divine assistance; whereas without such sacrifice and sub-
> missiveness great harm might ensue. The friends must
> be prepared to efface themselves at all times. Seeking the
> approval of men is many times the cause of imperiling
> the approval of God.[7]

Bahá'u'lláh has made the practice of consultation the
cornerstone of His new society. It involves ordinary people,
selected by democratic vote, given the responsibility to decide difficult matters and administer justice. But this does
not imply that there is no place for "experts" in this system.
The Bahá'í administrative order relies on both elected deci-
sion-makers and learned advisers. Assemblies are expected
to rely heavily on the advice of the members of the Continental Boards of Counselors and Auxiliary Board Mem-

bers. These are the "experts" on Bahá'í teachings, practices, and plans. But their role is only to advise and inspire. The decision-making authority rests with the democratically elected assemblies. In other matters Bahá'í assemblies are encouraged to consult as necessary with secular experts in every field: medicine and mental health, business and law, education, the arts, and science and engineering.

The Role of the Individual

Consultative bodies cannot always take the place of the motivated individual. Individual Bahá'ís, whether appointed to special positions or acting on their own, are often more effective than institutions at teaching the Faith and inspiring their Bahá'í brothers and sisters to action. The histories of all religions are replete with stories of individuals who arose and, overcoming all obstacles, accomplished incredible victories. But in the Bahá'í religion, the authority ultimately rests with the elected institutions, and individual initiative is most powerful when it is in concert with the shared plans and priorities of the group. This is accomplished through consultation: "The principle of consultation, which constitutes one of the basic laws of the Administration, should be applied to all Bahá'í activities that affect the collective interest of the Faith, for it is through cooperation and continued exchange of thoughts and views that the cause can best safeguard and foster its interests. Individual initiative, personal ability and resourcefulness, though indispensable, are, unless supported incapable of achieving such a tremendous task."[8]

Shoghi Effendi points out that Assemblies must be careful not to stifle individual initiative and freedom, and that individuals must be wise in their exercise of that freedom: "Let us also bear in mind that the keynote of the Cause of God [the Bahá'í Faith] is not dictatorial authority but humble fellowship, not arbitrary power, but the spirit of frank and loving consultation. Nothing short of the spirit of a true Bahá'í can hope to reconcile the principles of mercy and justice, of freedom and submission, of the sanctity of the right of the individual and of self-surrender, of vigilance, discretion and prudence on the one hand, and fellowship, candor, and courage on the other."[9]

Spiritual Maturity Revealed through Consultation

This is the fifth of the distinctive practices promoted by Bahá'u'lláh: that through the spiritual process of consultation, ordinary people can govern their affairs and solve difficult problems. The spiritual maturity of humankind, made possible in this age through God's will and blessing, is revealed when we consult: "Consultation bestoweth greater awareness and transmuteth conjecture into certitude. It is a shining light which, in a dark world, leadeth the way and guideth. For everything there is and will continue to be a station of perfection and maturity. The maturity of the gift of understanding is made manifest through consultation."[10]

It is obviously advantageous when those called upon to consult are intelligent, educated, and informed on the matters before them, but these are not requirements. Spiritual qualities are the requirement. 'Abdu'l-Bahá writes, "The prime requisites for them that take counsel together are purity of motive, radiance of spirit, detachment from all else save God, attraction to His divine fragrances, humility and lowliness amongst His loved ones, patience and long-suffering in difficulties and servitude to His exalted Threshold. Should they be graciously aided to acquire these attributes, victory from the unseen Kingdom of Bahá shall be vouchsafed to them."[11]

Shoghi Effendi says that, in voting for members of the Spiritual Assembly, spiritual attributes take precedence over material ones such as wealth or social position: "It is incumbent upon the chosen delegates to consider without the least trace of passion and prejudice, and irrespective of any material consideration, the names of only those who can best combine the necessary qualities of unquestioned loyalty, of selfless devotion, of a well-trained mind, of recognized ability and mature experience."[12]

It is through the method of consultation that Bahá'u'lláh has empowered His followers in every corner of the globe to take and adapt God's religion to their needs. This principle can be seen in His creation of the Universal House of Justice. In his Will and Testament, 'Abdu'l-Bahá gives this clear statement of the functioning of this institution (emphasis mine):

> It is incumbent upon these members [of the Universal House of Justice] to gather in a certain place and deliberate upon all problems which have caused difference, questions that are obscure and matters that are not expressly recorded in the Book [the writings of Bahá'u'lláh, specifically the Kitáb-i-Aqdas]. *Whatsoever they decide has the same*

effect as the Text itself. Inasmuch as the House of Justice hath power to enact laws that are not expressly recorded in the Book and bear upon daily transactions, so also it hath power to repeal the same. Thus for example, the House of Justice enacteth today a certain law and enforceth it, and a hundred years hence, circumstances having profoundly changed and the conditions having altered, another House of Justice will then have power, according to the exigencies of the time, to alter that law.*

The clear guidance is that this elected body, the House of Justice, is empowered to consult, decide, and act on any matter not covered in the holy writings, and at a later time, to alter its decision. While in effect, its decisions have the same authority as the writings of Bahá'u'lláh and 'Abdu'l-Bahá, but they are not permanent. They can be changed at any time by this same body. This system shows the great trust that Bahá'u'lláh places in His followers, first to elect nine people from their midst to be given this collective authority, then to trust the nine to consult and come to the correct decision, and finally for the believers to follow their decisions. Never before has a divine Manifestation turned over the reins of God's religion to the followers in a democratic system.

---

* 'Abdu'l-Bahá, Will and Testament, p. 20. Unlike other faiths, where time-honored religious practices and traditions have equal weight with the sacred texts and teachings of the Manifestation, in the Bahá'í religion the text is supreme. The body of scripture revealed by Bahá'u'lláh and its interpretation by 'Abdu'l-Bahá and Shoghi Effendi are fixed, until God chooses to supersede it with a new Manifestation. The House of Justice is empowered to add new provisions to meet new circumstances that arise but cannot override the sacred text and its interpretation.

10

Politics Is Shunned

One might expect that a religion so vitally concerned with the issues of peace, equality, and justice, and that anticipates the emergence of an effective system of international governance, would be actively involved in the world of everyday politics. This is not the case. Another of the distinctive teachings of the Bahá'í Faith is that, while Bahá'ís are loyal to their governments, political involvement is completely shunned. The Bahá'í plan is to gradually build a new society where decisions are made in a system free from political parties, constituencies, and individual leadership. This certainly seems a strange position to many Americans, who regard the confrontational and divisive methods of politics as a natural and even divinely sanctioned way of making decisions and taking collective action.

Loyalty Yet Noninvolvement

Bahá'u'lláh and 'Abdu'l-Bahá both make it clear that Bahá'ís are to be obedient to their respective governments: "O ye beloved of the Lord! It is incumbent upon you to be submissive to all monarchs that are just and to show your fidelity to every righteous king. Serve ye the sovereigns of the world with utmost truthfulness and loyalty. Show obedience unto them and be their well-wishers. Without their leave and permission do not meddle with political affairs, for disloyalty to the just sovereign is disloyalty to God Him-self."[1] But they must not forget that their mission is essen-tially a spiritual one, and becoming involved in political issues is not prudent:

> Religious matters should not be confused with politics in the present state of the world (for their interests are not identical).
>
> Religion concerns matters of the heart, of the spirit, and of morals.
>
> Politics are occupied with the material things of life. Religious teachers should not invade the realm of politics; they should concern themselves with the spiritual educa-tion of the people; they should ever give good counsel to men, trying to serve God and human kind; they should endeavor to awaken spiritual aspiration, and strive to en-large the understanding and knowledge of humanity, to improve morals, and to increase the love for justice.
>
> This is in accordance with the Teaching of Bahá'u'lláh. In the Gospel also it is written, "Render unto Caesar the things which are Caesar's, and unto God the things which are God's."[2]

Shoghi Effendi expands on this subject in many letters, and makes it clear that Bahá'ís have no latitude to decide which governments are just or unjust:

> The attitude of the Bahá'ís must be two-fold, com-plete obedience to the government of the country they reside in, and no interference whatsoever in political

matters or questions. What the Master's ['Abdu'l-Bahá's] statement really means is obedience to a duly constituted government, whatever that government may be in form. We are not the ones, as individual Bahá'ís, to judge our government as just or unjust—for each believer would be sure to hold a different viewpoint, and within our own Bahá'í fold a hotbed of dissension would spring up and destroy our unity. We must build up our own Bahá'í system, and leave the faulty systems of the world to go their way.[3]

Bahá'ís are expected to be loyal to their government, up to the point of recanting their Faith. That they will not do: "We see therefore that we must do two things—Shun politics like the plague, and be obedient to the Government in power in the place where we reside. . . . We must obey in all cases except where a spiritual principle is involved, such as denying our Faith. For these spiritual principles we must be willing to die."[4]

What are the reasons for this twofold teaching of loyalty yet noninvolvement? As the quotation above reveals, the first priority of the Bahá'ís is to build a new system, a new civilization. Involvement in politics is at best a distraction from this mission, and at worst the potential source of disunity among the Bahá'ís themselves. The unity made possible by the Bahá'í Covenant and its administrative order, as discussed in chapter 6, is too precious to risk.

A second, more practical reason for avoiding politics is that the worldwide Bahá'í community is represented in nearly every nation and territory of the earth. In some of these, primarily in the Islamic world, the Bahá'ís are under severe restrictions. Most of their religious activities and meetings are forbidden. In a few places, they are in physical danger because of their beliefs. Any apparent connection between the Bahá'í Faith and political activities in another country may unleash even greater persecutions upon them.

The Real Solution

Bahá'í noninvolvement in politics is sometimes misunderstood as disinterest in or aloofness from the "real" issues and problems of today. Contrary to this, Bahá'ís are free to vote in any election where they can do so without identifying themselves as members of a political party. They are free to approach their elected representatives with their concerns and ideas. They serve with loyalty in nonpolitical and civil service positions. They are even free to run for office, provided they are not associated with a party. They are free to join peaceful protests as their conscience moves them. But their central mission, the building of a new society based on unity and justice, they see as fundamental to the long term and permanent solutions of the world's problems. And while there are plenty of people ready to work on the immediate problems (usually by trying to get others to change *their* ways), only the Bahá'ís are working on what they believe to be the *real* problem, the lack of true unity among peoples, by first changing themselves. This is the sixth distinctive practice. Bahá'ís believe working on true unity is fundamentally more important than solving more obvious problems.

As mentioned in chapter 3, during the years of His exile in Adrianople, Bahá'u'lláh wrote a series of letters to the rulers of His time, urging them to rule with justice, settle their differences and put an end to war. Recently, the Universal House of Justice has addressed the rulers of today with a new series of letters, forcefully stating the Bahá'í view that the world's great problems stem from a lack of unity. Anyone interested in learning what the Bahá'í Faith teaches about the problems of today should study these letters. The best known of these is *The Promise of World Peace* (1985), which outlines the Bahá'í view on the relationship between peace, unity, and justice; some of the points raised by this letter were discussed in chapter 3. In 2002, a letter from the Universal House of Justice addressed to the world's religious leaders, called them to abandon fundamentalism and narrow self interest, and by embracing interfaith dialogue and tolerance, to reclaim their position of moral and spiritual leadership.

Other documents, such as statements issued by the Bahá'í International Community (see the next section), contribute to the ongoing process of making known the Bahá'í positions on important issues. For example, *Turning Point for All Nations* (1995) offers the Bahá'í perspective on the successes and shortcomings of the first fifty years of the United Nations and *The Prosperity of Humankind* (1995) addresses the need for a new approach to issues of economic and social development (which is taken up in chapter 13).

Support for International Organizations

While Bahá'ís avoid all partisan political entanglements, they do cooperate with international nonpartisan organizations with similar goals and visions. The key is to use wisdom:

As you are aware, it is not the practice of Bahá'í institutions or individuals to take positions on the political decisions of governments. . . . The central importance of the principle of avoidance of politics and controversial matters is that Bahá'ís should not allow themselves to be involved in the disputes of the many conflicting elements of the society around them. The aim of the Bahá'ís is to reconcile viewpoints, to heal divisions, and to bring about tolerance and mutual respect among men, and this aim is undermined if we allow ourselves to be swept along by the ephemeral passions of others. This does not mean that Bahá'ís cannot collaborate with any non-Bahá'í movement; it does mean that good judgment is required to distinguish those activities and associations which are beneficial and constructive from those which are divisive.[5]

The Bahá'ís, as also mentioned in chapter 3, have a long history of cooperation and support of international peace movements that are nonpartisan in nature. Their relationship with the United Nations is the best example. Since 1948, the Bahá'í Faith has maintained an official presence at the United Nations, as an international nongovernmental organization (NGO) known as the *Bahá'í International Community* (*BIC*). It is now an agency of the Universal House of Justice. This office is actively involved both in representing the Bahá'í interests to the UN and in making the Bahá'í positions on important issues known to the UN and its agencies. Some of the issues on which position papers have been prepared are human rights, the rights of women and girls, universal education, elimination of torture, the rights of minorities, economic and social development, drug abuse, environmental responsibility, and the elimination of poverty. The Bahá'í International Community is an active participant in global and regional UN conferences on these issues.

In 1970 the BIC received consultative status with the UN Economic and Social Council; in 1974 it became formally associated with the UN Environment Programme, and in 1976 it gained consultative status with the UN Children's Fund. During the years that followed, the BIC has become highly regarded within the UN as a nonpartisan voice for human rights, peace, and progress. It had a prominent place in the 1990 World Conference on Education for All, the 1990 World Summit for Children, the 1992 UN Conference on the Environment (the "Earth Summit"), the 1993 World Conference on Human Rights, the 1994 International Conference on Population, the 1995 World Summit for Development, the 1995 Fourth World Conference on Women, the Millennium Forum, the 2001 World Conference against Racism, and many other major international forums.

The worldwide Bahá'í community has also benefited from the international legal structure that has evolved in the last eighty years. From time to time, when the Bahá'ís were under extreme pressure and restrictions by authorities in a few Islamic nations, it has been able to appeal to such entities as the League of Nations Permanent Mandates Commission and the UN Human Rights Commission. These bodies have often been successful in stemming the tide of persecution against fragile minority communities.

One hundred and forty years ago, Bahá'u'lláh said that the existing world was pregnant with a new civilization, and called on the leaders of the world not to resist the birth process but to assist it by coming together and settling their differences, ruling with justice, and putting an end to war. To this point they have ignored this call, and the labor pains continue, becoming worse with each generation. Eventually, they will have no choice but to move forward. It is the mission of the Bahá'ís to show them the direction.

11

Work, Art, Money,
Service, and Sacrifice

One of the "proofs" of the divine origin of a Manifestation of God, as discussed in chapter 2, is that His teachings lead to the building of a great civilization, where daily life reflects the principles He put forth. Bahá'u'lláh brings new teachings that spiritualize the everyday life of His followers.

Service to Humankind

The Bahá'í writings reaffirm Christ's pronouncement that, in the Kingdom of God, the greatest among us will be our servant.[1] The station of servitude to humanity is the highest a Bahá'í can attain. Along with virtue, it gives the true measure of each person's worth: "Man's merit lieth in service and virtue and not in the pageantry of wealth and riches."[2]

The life of 'Abdu'l-Bahá, a title that literally means "servant of Bahá'u'lláh," is the example to which Bahá'ís aspire. After his father's death, 'Abdu'l-Bahá made it clear that service to his father's mission was his only purpose: "My name is 'Abdu'l-Bahá, my identity is 'Abdu'l-Bahá, my qualification is 'Abdu'l-Bahá, my reality is 'Abdu'l-Bahá, my praise is 'Abdu'l-Bahá. Thralldom to the Blessed Perfection [Bahá'u'lláh] is my glorious refulgent diadem; and servitude to all the human race is my perpetual religion. . . . No name, no title, no mention, no commendation hath he nor will ever have except 'Abdu'l-Bahá. This is my longing. This is my supreme apex. This is my greatest yearning. This is my eternal life. This is my everlasting glory!"[3]

Statements such as these will not be at all strange to the followers of any of the world's faiths. Humble service to God and humanity has always been one of their hallmarks. But every Manifestation of God, in keeping with His plan for that place and time, instills into humanity a new spiritual capacity, and the outward form of religion must be altered to conform. This new capacity, like any empty vessel, can be used for either good or evil, creation or destruction. Bahá'u'lláh's revelation creates within all people the nascent faculty I have called the eye of oneness, and gives the specific teachings designed to steer humanity toward the positive use of this power.

The Universal House of Justice explains that the station and importance of service is greater now than ever before:

> Together with the crumbling of barriers separating peoples, our age is witnessing the dissolution of the once insuperable wall that the past assumed would forever separate the life of Heaven from the life of Earth. The scriptures of all religions have always taught the believer to see in service to others not only a moral duty, but an avenue for the soul's own approach to God. Today, the progressive restructuring of society gives this familiar teaching new dimensions of meaning. As the age-old promise of a world animated by principles of justice slowly takes on the character of a realistic goal, meeting the needs

of the soul and those of society will increasingly be seen as reciprocal aspects of a mature spiritual life.[4]

The rest of this chapter explores several areas in which Bahá-'u'lláh unites through service the spiritual and the practical dimension of life.

Work Is Worship

In chapter 9 it was explained that the Bahá'í teachings elevate decision-making to the status of a spiritual activity. Bahá'u'lláh also elevates work, especially when performed in the spirit of service, to the status of worship of God. In the Kitáb-i-Aqdas, Bahá'u'lláh writes that not only is work worship, but not working is unacceptable:

> O people of Bahá! It is incumbent upon each one of you to engage in some occupation—such as a craft, a trade or the like. We have exalted your engagement in such work to the rank of worship of the one true God. Reflect, O people, on the grace and blessings of your Lord, and yield Him thanks at eventide and dawn. Waste not your hours in idleness and sloth, but occupy yourselves with what will profit you and others. Thus hath it been decreed in this Tablet from whose horizon hath shone the day-star of wisdom and utterance.[5]

The wording of this passage suggests that formal, paid work is considered worship, but other writings make it clear that the spirit of service makes any labor equivalent to worship. For instance, a parent who stays at home to raise children, or a retiree or person of means who is engaged in service to the community, is worshiping God by their "work." Nor is it what you do that makes work equivalent to worship; it is the spirit in which it is done. Most people do not get to choose what work they must do on a day to day basis. Some are fortunate enough to be employed in positions of direct service to people, communities, or nations. Others must work in the background, several steps removed from the final beneficiary of their labors. This does not prevent their work from being performed "in the spirit of service."

Beauty Is Essential

Art and music are also singled out by Bahá'u'lláh as expressions that, when undertaken in this same spirit, are equivalent to worship. What's more, they have a profound effect on people's souls and are an effective means for attracting people to the Bahá'í teachings, for creating spirituality and building unity within the Bahá'í community. Bahá'í artists are free to work in whatever style or mode they and their community find comfortable; there is no such thing at this time as Bahá'í styles of art, music, literature, or architecture. They eagerly explore the implications of the oneness of humanity for artistic expression.

Bahá'u'lláh teaches that beauty is essential for spiritual life. It is not an optional accessory that can be added at some later time, budget permitting. Visiting any of the Bahá'í Houses of Worship around the world, or the Bahá'í properties in Haifa and Acre, Israel, will demonstrate that beauty and dignity are of the highest importance and must enter into consideration in any project.

Art and music are, almost by definition, infused into Bahá'í worship and devotions. In several places, Bahá'u'lláh says that the prayers and sacred writings are more potent when they are chanted or intoned: "They who recite the verses of the All-Merciful in the most melodious of tones will perceive in them that with which the sovereignty of earth and heaven can never be compared. From them they will inhale the divine fragrance of My worlds—worlds which today none can discern save those who have been endowed with vision through this sublime, this beauteous Revelation. Say: These verses draw hearts that are pure unto those spiritual worlds that can neither be expressed in words nor intimated by allusion. Blessed are those who hearken."* Chanting or intoning prayer is a practice that people from many cultures and religious traditions are comfortable with, but one that most Americans from mainstream Protestant backgrounds find new and challenging. Again, there is no uniform Bahá'í way of incorporating the arts into worship; people are free to explore and develop their own approaches.

The Responsibilities of Wealth

By regarding work and art as expressions of worship, Bahá'u'lláh has raised the bar for His followers. It is no longer

---

* Bahá'u'lláh, Kitáb-i-Aqdas, ¶116. In their original languages, many of Bahá'u'lláh's prayers and writings, including the Kitáb-i-Aqdas itself, have the meter and often the rhyme of poetry, and are often chanted in those languages.

acceptable to be idly rich, or idly poor. Everyone is to support themselves and their families to whatever degree is possible, and to be a servant to humanity. Those who are wealthy have a special responsibility to the community: to support those who cannot support themselves. Bahá'u'lláh asserts that the rich have the poor "in their trust," and that God is watching: "O Ye Rich Ones On Earth! The poor in your midst are My trust; guard ye My trust, and be not intent only on your own ease."[6]

Bahá'ís are instructed to have a spiritual attitude toward money and wealth. It is not evil to be wealthy, but wealth can be a dangerous trap to the spirit:

> O Ye That Pride Yourselves On Mortal Riches! Know ye in truth that wealth is a mighty barrier between the seeker and his desire [God], the lover and his beloved. The rich, but for a few, shall in no wise attain the court of His presence nor enter the city of content and resignation. Well is it then with him, who, being rich, is not hindered by his riches from the eternal kingdom, nor deprived by them of imperishable dominion. By the Most Great Name! The splendor of such a wealthy man shall illuminate the dwellers of heaven even as the sun enlightens the people of the earth![7]

They are expected to be moderate, not extravagant, in their use of wealth, but need not deprive themselves of every comfort:

> Should a man wish to adorn himself with the ornaments of the earth, to wear its apparels, or partake of the benefits

it can bestow, no harm can befall him, if he alloweth nothing whatever to intervene between him and God, for God hath ordained every good thing, whether created in the heavens or in the earth, for such of His servants as truly believe in Him. Eat ye, O people, of the good things which God hath allowed you, and deprive not yourselves from His wondrous bounties. Render thanks and praise unto Him, and be of them that are truly thankful.[8]

And Bahá'ís are expected to be charitable, to help those less fortunate and in need: "Charity is pleasing and praiseworthy in the sight of God and is regarded as a prince among goodly deeds."[9] They are to follow the example of 'Abdu'l-Bahá, who, like his father, was known all his life as a champion and sustainer of the poor and powerless.* The Bahá'í writings call for "the elimination of the extremes of wealth and poverty." But charity alone will not solve the problem of world poverty. That requires a new, global society where economic relationships are just and people see themselves as the members of one organic human family, in which both rich and poor have responsibilities: the rich to be charitable and the poor to work for their own self-sufficiency. This is what Bahá'ís mean when they say there must be "a spiritual solution to the economic problem."

It is not possible for individual Bahá'ís, or their communities, to respond to every valid request for material assistance. But spiritual assistance is also important. Bahá'u'lláh

---

* 'Abdu'l-Bahá was knighted by the British government in 1920, in part for His work to grow and distribute food to the starving residents of Palestine during World War I.

instructs them to be aware of the plight of their fellows, to listen to their stories and view them with empathy even if they cannot solve their problems materially: "O Children of Dust! Tell the rich of the midnight sighing of the poor, lest heedlessness lead them into the path of destruction, and deprive them of the Tree of Wealth. To give and to be generous are attributes of Mine; well is it with him that adorneth himself with My virtues."[10]

To give and to be generous are virtues of God, and every person, whether they are rich or poor, should try to acquire all the divine virtues. In another place He writes that spiritual blessings will descend on those who befriend the less fortunate:

> If ye meet the abased or the down-trodden, turn not away disdainfully from them, for the King of Glory ever watcheth over them and surroundeth them with such tenderness as none can fathom except them that have suffered their wishes and desires to be merged in the Will of your Lord, the Gracious, the All-Wise. O ye rich ones of the earth! Flee not from the face of the poor that lieth in the dust, nay rather befriend him and suffer him to recount the tale of the woes with which God's inscrutable Decree hath caused him to be afflicted. By the righteousness of God! Whilst ye consort with him, the Concourse on high will be looking upon you, will be interceding for you, will be extolling your names and glorifying your action. Blessed are the learned that pride not themselves on their attainments; and well is it with the righteous that mock not the sinful, but rather conceal their misdeeds, so that their own shortcomings may remain veiled to men's eyes.[11]

A particular sort of charity is given special significance by Bahá'u'lláh: the education of the children of the poor. If someone takes it upon himself to educate one of them, it is as if he educated one of Bahá'u'lláh's own children.

Material Support of the Bahá'í Faith

A charitable act all Bahá'ís can perform is to contribute to the funds that support the activities of their religion. There are separate funds for local, national, and international activities, and a fund to support the work of the Continental Counselors. From time to time there may be funds set up for special projects. In keeping with the Bahá'í view of maturity, there are no standards for the amount anyone should contribute, nor is anyone ever singled out for supporting, or not supporting, the Bahá'í funds. This matter is strictly between the individual and God. The funds are used only to do the work of the Bahá'í Faith, and only Bahá'ís may contribute to them.

Bahá'ís are expected to manage their material wealth wisely, whether it is great or small. Besides the exhortation to work and support oneself, the Kitáb-i-Aqdas also instructs them to provide for the support of their families and the education of their children, the children of the poor, and to make a will that fairly distributes the wealth accumulated in a lifetime. A special fund, established by Bahá'u'lláh in the Kitáb-i-Aqdas, is the *Ḥuqúqu'lláh,* or *Right of God.* This is a tax of nineteen percent on whatever wealth a Bahá'í acquires beyond what is needed for ordinary expenses and modest savings. More important than the mechanics of calculation are the spiritual principles behind it. While the Right of God is obligatory for Bahá'ís, it relies on voluntary compliance. There are never any solicitations; it depends on the maturity of the individual to compute and pay what she owes. Bahá'u'lláh promises blessings to those who comply with a spirit of joy:

> It is clear and evident that the payment of the Right of God is conducive to prosperity, to blessing, and to honor and divine protection. Well is it with them that comprehend and recognize this truth and woe betide them that believe not. And this is on condition that the individual should observe the injunctions prescribed in the Book with the utmost radiance, gladness and willing acquiescence. It behooveth you to counsel the friends to do that which is right and praiseworthy. Whoso hearkeneth to this call, it is to his own behoof, and whoso faileth bringeth loss upon himself. Verily our Lord of Mercy is the All-Sufficing, the All-Praised.[12]

The money rendered through this fund is administered by the House of Justice. It is used for projects and humanitarian needs throughout the world.

The Mystery of Sacrifice

Another sign of the maturity that Bahá'u'lláh expects from his followers is that they are free to seek their own balance between work and leisure, wealth and poverty, rest and service. It is not God's desire that one should work until she is ill, or to give away everything she owns. Yet there is a special, spiritual dynamic involved in sacrifice, what the Bahá'í writings call the "mystery of sacrifice," whereby God rewards those who go above and beyond. Of course, the foundations of all religions are built on sacrifice; first by the Manifestations themselves, who invariably suffered ridicule, persecution, and often death, then by their first followers who often chose to trade their lives for the joy of embracing God's new message. In the Bábí and Bahá'í religions, the Báb met His end by firing squad, Bahá'u'lláh and 'Abdu'l-Bahá spent most of their lives as prisoners. Bahá'u'lláh's youngest son, Mírzá Mihdí, died at the age of twenty-two, shortly after the family's exile to the prison fortress of Acre; later the infant sons of 'Abdu'l-Bahá died in the same city. Over twenty thousand of the early Bábí and Bahá'í believers were killed because of their allegiance to their new Faith. These sacrifices, Bahá'u'lláh assures His followers, are rewarded in God's spiritual worlds, and are the cause of progress in this world.

Today, most Bahá'ís in the West are not asked to risk their lives for their Faith, but they are still called upon to give of themselves sacrificially for its advancement. Each Bahá'í must decide for himself what he can sacrifice. One may give up his home and career path to serve as a pioneer in another land; others commit to serving long hours on Bahá'í institutions, either elected or appointed, or to facilitating classes for children or youth, opening their homes for meetings, or serving in countless other ways. It is not for anyone to judge the degree of sacrifice and service offered by another.

A study of the Bahá'í writings on the mystery of sacrifice would require a book of its own. Their basis lies, once more, in the belief that man is a spiritual being. To sacrifice is to put aside the lower concerns of the material world and focus on the higher concerns—what God asks of us. Every time we do this, we receive bounties and blessings, and it becomes easier. Our own consciousness of our spiritual nature becomes stronger, and we can take bigger steps with more confidence. Religion teaches that the material and spiritual world are intimately connected and intertwined. This is the seventh distinguishing practice of the Bahá'í Faith: Everyday human concerns such as education, work, art, time, and money, when viewed with the eye of oneness, are really spiritual concerns and how we manage them has great importance for our own spiritual lives and the well-being of the world. Things are much more interconnected than they might seem.

12

The Power of Youth

In 1844, the Báb spoke to His disciples of the day coming soon, when "Him whom God shall make manifest" will arise. He prophesied that, "The newly born babe of that Day excels the wisest and most venerable men of this time."[1] One hundred and sixty years later, this prophecy is being fulfilled by Bahá'í children and youth around the world.

Bahá'í Youth Can Move the World

Since its inception, youth and young adults have been central in the development and spread of the Bahá'í religion. The Báb was only twenty-five years old when He began His ministry; many of His first eighteen disciples, called the *Letters of the Living*, were younger still. 'Abdu'l-Bahá was only nine when he accompanied his father into exile and began his life of service. Shoghi Effendi was twenty-two and a university student when he became Guardian after his grandfather's passing. Today, youth continue to make remarkable contributions and great sacrifices, and must be regarded among the "spiritual leaders" of the Bahá'í community.*

---

* In the wake of the 1979 Islamic Revolution in Iran, many Bahá'í youth, both men and women, were imprisoned and several were executed in an attempt to deprive the Bahá'í community of its leadership.

The eighth distinguishing practice of the Bahá'ís is this: They expect their children and youth, irrespective of their biological age, to be spiritually mature members of Bahá-'u'lláh's new race of men. They believe that children and youth have extraordinary capabilities for knowledge, wisdom, action, and sacrifice far beyond what Western society understands and expects from its young people.

What are the powers and forces that enable Bahá'í youth to make these contributions and sacrifices? In many ways, Bahá'í youth are no different from the young people of any other community. They are blessed with energy at a time in their lives when they have the flexibility to take advantage of opportunities.

But there are important differences as well. First, many Bahá'í children have the advantage of growing up in a warm and nurturing community that values them highly and invests in their development. They get to spend at least a portion of their time in an atmosphere that discourages materialism, backbiting, gossip, faultfinding, and criticism, and encourages love, support, and working in groups. They associate with people of different races, nationalities, and customs, and have the opportunity to develop their own eye of oneness. They are instilled with the idea that they truly are world citizens. In Bahá'í children's classes they are taught not only the tenets of their Faith, but to respect the divine origin and reality of all the world's great religions, to understand, memorize, and recite the prayers and sacred scriptures, and to explain the Bahá'í teachings to their peers. They are coached to stand before an audience and give eloquent and poised presentations. As they become older, they have the opportunity to participate in special gatherings for children, junior youth and youth, such as summer schools, retreats, conferences, and projects, where their Bahá'í identity and wisdom will be further strengthened.

Starting life as a Bahá'í child means that a young person can, perhaps, avoid some of the mistakes of his elders. The standard of morality—the "rectitude of conduct" and "chaste and holy life" described by Shoghi Effendi—may seem impossibly high to many adults, but is readily achieved by young people who see in their Faith an alternative to racial division and distrust, the poisonous atmosphere created by gossip and backbiting, and the smothering effects of material culture and authoritarian systems.

A second advantage is the priority on ensuring that Bahá'í children are educated. Bahá'í families and communities value education and encourage young people to excel in their studies. This encouragement, along with positive attitudes toward work, service, art, and science, interest in and concern about the peoples of the world, and belief in the fundamental worth of the individual, combine to create motivated students. A positive attitude toward learning can be found all over the Bahá'í world, in cultures that already value education highly and those that do not. Bahá'í children are often exceptional students.

A third advantage that Bahá'í youth enjoy is being in a community that cultivates a personal sense of spirituality. Bahá'u'lláh has identified the age of fifteen as the beginning of maturity. It is at about this time that all young people, but especially Bahá'í youth, begin the process of independent investigation of truth. The idea of spirituality is not strange to them. They can see how a spiritual foundation influences the rest of life. They can study the sacred writings for themselves, ask serious questions of their peers and elders, and take ownership of their own spiritual growth and development through regular prayer. At this age they will be making important decisions that will affect the rest of their lives.

An avenue for Bahá'í youth to develop and express their spirituality is through the arts. The arts, as discussed in the last chapter, are considered an expression of worship. Youth in particular find them a profound medium of communication with their peers. In many Bahá'í communities groups known as *youth workshops* have been formed. These employ the visual and performing arts, especially dance and music, to convey the Bahá'í teachings of the oneness and wholeness of humanity. There are youth workshops in many countries and regions, each adapting their message to the audience and their medium to the artistic forms of their culture. Non-Bahá'í youth are welcome participants in most of these workshops.

A fourth distinction is that Bahá'í youth see their lives as instruments of service to their Faith and humanity. As they become firm in commitment to their religion, the House of Justice says that there are three general paths of service they must try to integrate into their lives:

> First, the foundation of all their accomplishments, is their study of the teachings, the spiritualization of their lives, and the forming of their characters in accordance with the standards of Bahá'u'lláh. . . . The life of a Bahá'í

will be characterized by truthfulness and decency; he will walk uprightly among his fellowmen, dependent upon none save God, yet linked by bonds of love and brotherhood with mankind; he will be entirely detached from the loose standards, the decadent theories, the frenetic experimentation, the desperation of present-day society, will look upon his neighbors with a bright and friendly face, and be a beacon of light and haven for all those who would emulate his strength of character and assurance of soul.

The second field of service, which is linked intimately with the first, is teaching the Faith, particularly to their fellow youth, among whom are some of the most open and seeking minds in the world. Not yet having acquired all the responsibilities of a family or a long-established home and job, youth can the more easily choose where they will live and study or work. . . . Bahá'í youth, bearing the incomparable treasure of the Word of God for this Day, can harness this mobility into service for mankind and can choose their places of residence, their areas of travel, and their types of work with the goal in mind of how they can best serve the Faith.

The third field of service is the preparation by youth for their later years. It is the obligation of a Bahá'í to educate his children; likewise it is the duty of the children to acquire knowledge of the arts and sciences and to learn a trade or a profession whereby they, in turn, can earn their living and support their families. This, for a Bahá'í youth, is in itself a service to God, a service, moreover, which can be combined with teaching the Faith and often with pioneering. The Bahá'í community will need men and women of many skills and qualifications; for, as it grows in size the sphere of its activities in the life of society will increase and diversify. Let Bahá'í youth, therefore, consider the best ways in which they can use and develop their native abilities for the service of mankind and the Cause of God, whether this be as farmers, teachers, doctors, artisans, musicians, or any one of the multitude of livelihoods that are open to them.[2]

It is common for children and youth to be active members of committees and projects within their local communities, and to be engaged in consultation with other Bahá'ís of all ages.

There are also special avenues of service and opportunity open to Bahá'í youth. Since young people in the United States and other first world countries often have their summers free, they have the opportunity to participate in extended projects of service. These may be close to home or international. Participation in an international project gives them an opportunity to practice their language skills, learn about another society, and see the worldwide Bahá'í community in operation. The past thirty years in particular have seen the rise of what has been called an international Bahá'í youth culture, with young adults from many parts of the world in contact and communication, sharing their successes and trials.

A unique service opportunity is the *Youth Year of Service* program. Young Bahá'ís have the option of taking a full year, usually before starting college, to serve at an assignment such as a Bahá'í school or development project (see chapter 13). Like summer projects, these may be at home or abroad. This year, especially if served internationally, helps to build a broad and mature outlook, independence, and self reliance, and may go on to affect the young person's career and life choices from that point forward. This year of service is optional, and each young person should consult with his parents and Spiritual Assembly to determine if it is the appropriate choice.

A final advantage held by Bahá'í youth is that they are expected to challenge their elders. They can more easily see the gap between the promise of Bahá'u'lláh's new society and what has been accomplished so far. They are often able to respond more eagerly to new ideas. The Universal House of Justice writes, "The spirit of zeal and enthusiasm characteristic of youth has also provided an ongoing challenge to the general body of the community to explore ever more audaciously the revolutionary social implications of Bahá-'u'lláh's teachings."[3]

Young people are not deceived by lofty words and ideals that do not lead to action; neither is God. An example of this in the United States has been the development of the study circle as a method of Bahá'í education (see chapter 15). Youth have been at the forefront of those responding to the call of the House of Justice to engage in study circles and become facilitators. They find the learning culture model of consultation, action, and reflection to be very natural.

Bahá'í youth around the world are responding to Bahá-'u'lláh's call to build a new civilization free from hate, division, and injustice. They are not interested in being told what can't be done. The House of Justice gives them these words of encouragement:

Be not dismayed if your endeavors are dismissed as utopian by the voices that would oppose any suggestion of fundamental change. Trust in the capacity of this generation to disentangle itself from the embroilments of a divided society. To discharge your responsibilities, you will have to show forth courage, the courage of those who cling to standards of rectitude, whose lives are characterized by purity of thought and action, and whose purpose is directed by love and indomitable faith. As you dedicate yourselves to healing the wounds with which your peoples have been afflicted, you will become invincible champions of justice.[4]

The High Station of the Educator

Of all the roles and stations of the Manifestations of God, the role of "divine educator" is perhaps the most prominent in the Bahá'í texts. The theme of education, both spiritual and material, has already arisen many times in this book, and more are to come. The gap between the disordered world of today and the ordered world of the future can only be bridged by one thing, and that is education. I believe that in the not-too-distant future, the Bahá'í religion will become known as the religion of education.

Bahá'u'lláh says that the education of children is a universal requirement of this time, and the nature and significance of education is discussed at great length in the Bahá'í writings. First the mother has the responsibility to guide and train the child from infancy; then the father and the community are required to see that the child receives a formal education, and finally the young person himself takes on the obligation of learning a trade or profession, which the House of Justice says is "in itself a service to God." Spiritual education, in the form of reading and study of the sacred scriptures, is a lifelong process.

It should come as no surprise therefore that the position of educator is held in high regard in the Bahá'í writings. Whether as a mother, a teacher of Bahá'í children's classes, or a professional teacher, the role of the educator and the act of educating is one of the highest forms of service and most noble endeavors of humankind. Concerning the mother's duty to educate her children, 'Abdu'l-Bahá writes, "O ye loving mothers, know ye that in God's sight, the best of all ways to worship Him is to educate the children and train them in all the perfections of humankind; and no nobler deed than this can be imagined."[5] Similar passages heap praise on the other teachers in a child's life.

In His holy book, the Bayán, the Báb requests that His followers prepare a will to distribute their material wealth at death, and gives a formula for an ideal distribution among heirs. Bahá'u'lláh, in the Kitáb-i-Aqdas, reaffirms most of His predecessor's provisions in this matter, giving proportions that should go to spouses, children, parents, brothers, and sisters. The only persons outside of the immediate family who are included in this distribution are one's teachers, who are entitled to approximately a 7 percent share. This is just one indication of the supreme importance of education and the high station of educators in the Bahá'í religion.

The Bahá'í writings make a distinction between material and spiritual education. While they are both enjoined by

Bahá'u'lláh, they must be in balance, and it is not accept-able to emphasize the academic subjects at the expense of spiritual and moral education. 'Abdu'l-Bahá writes that moral education is actually more important for the progress of the world:

> Training in morals and good conduct is far more im-portant than book learning. A child that is cleanly, agree-able, of good character, well-behaved—even though he be ignorant—is preferable to a child that is rude, unwashed, ill-natured, and yet becoming deeply versed in all the sci-ences and arts. The reason for this is that the child who conducts himself well, even though he be ignorant, is of benefit to others, while an ill-natured, ill-behaved child is corrupted and harmful to others, even though he be learned. If, however, the child be trained to be both learned and good, the result is light upon light.[6]

Bahá'í children and youth, having both moral and academic education, are typically "light upon light."

13

Social and Economic Development

Chapter 11 explored why, for Bahá'ís, service to humanity is a natural expression of their faith. Bahá'u'lláh calls on His followers to be active in solving the problems of the world's peoples: "Be anxiously concerned with the needs of the age ye live in, and center your deliberations on its exigencies and requirements."[1] This they manifest with a proactive, spiritually based approach to material progress.

Material and Spiritual Development

At the time of the inception of the Bahá'í religion, its birthplace of Persia was one of the most repressive, superstitious, fanatical, and politically corrupt places in the world. In 1875, Bahá'u'lláh instructed 'Abdu'l-Bahá, who was then thirty-one years of age, to write an open letter to the people of Persia, advising them on the steps necessary to put their nation on the road to progress and development. This letter was later translated and published under the title *The Secret of Divine Civilization*. "O people of Persia!" it asks, "How long will you wander? How long must your confusion last? How long will it go on, this conflict of opinions, this useless antagonism, this ignorance, this refusal to think? Others are alert, and we sleep our dreamless sleep. Other nations are making every effort to improve their condition; we are trapped in our desires and self-indulgences, and at every step we stumble into a new snare."[2] This treatise is too long to summarize here, but its central message is that the material progress of a community is founded on the spiritual development of the individual, that people must arise from their slumber and begin the process of spiritual and intellectual development. Once individuals can stand on their own feet, they can consult and seek justice and prosperity.

The ills afflicting humanity are many and complex. Thousands of institutions exist to address these problems at the local, national, and international levels. What is different in the Bahá'í approach is that they believe, as 'Abdu'l-Bahá stated, that these problems are fundamentally spiritual, not material. Purely material approaches will lead to at best temporary solutions, unless the people involved have an allegiance to moral values, education, human rights, justice, the oneness of humankind, and the value of every person.

Bahá'u'lláh established an institution to serve as a model for this view of development, the *House of Worship*. At the center of this institution is the physical building called the House of Worship, a temple that is an expression of man's spiritual core and orientation—its Arabic name, Mashriqu'l-Adhkár, literally means "dawning place of the remembrance of God." It is surrounded with other institutions, called *dependencies*, that address the material needs of society, such as schools and universities, hospitals, libraries, and charitable services for the poor, disabled, aged, orphans, and the needy, which are open to the followers of all faiths. Together this complex is the institution of the House of Worship, which is to be established in every city, according to Bahá'u'lláh's command.

Promoting Programs of Social and Economic Development

Establishing Houses of Worship and their dependencies requires human and capital resources beyond the capacities of current Bahá'í communities in most cities. While a limited number of Houses of Worship (the temple itself) and some of their dependencies have been built around the world, Bahá'ís in every country are moving toward Bahá'u'lláh's vision by creating projects for meeting humanity's material needs. These projects of social and economic development draw their inspiration from Bahá'u'lláh's proclamation that "the progress of the world" and "the development of nations" are part of God's plan for today, from the model of the House of Worship, and from 'Abdu'l-Bahá's writings and the example of his life of service.

In 1983 the Universal House of Justice, noting that material progress is one of God's wishes for today, established an Office of Social and Economic Development to assist the Bahá'ís throughout the world, especially in third world nations, to create their own plans for development: "Now, after all the years of constant teaching activity, the Community of the Greatest Name [the Bahá'í community] has grown to the stage at which the processes of this development must be incorporated into its regular pursuits; particularly is action compelled by the expansion of the Faith in third world countries where the vast majority of its adherents reside."[3] Unlike many development projects, which are conceived and instituted from the top down, the Bahá'í model of social and economic development is one of grassroots activity, born out of consultation and carried out through local action. The House of Justice calls on the National Spiritual Assemblies in each country to be a catalyst for these programs:

> Progress in the development field will largely depend on natural stirrings at the grassroots, and it should receive its driving force from those sources rather than from an imposition of plans and programs from the top. The major task of National Assemblies, therefore, is to increase the local communities' awareness of needs and possibilities, and to guide and coordinate the efforts resulting from such awareness. Already in many areas the friends are witnessing the confirmations of their initiatives in such pursuits as the founding of tutorial and other schools, the promotion of literacy, the launching of rural development programs, the inception of educational radio stations, and the operation of agricultural and medical projects. As they enlarge the scope of their endeavors other modes of development will undoubtedly emerge.[4]

As was explored in chapter 9, Bahá'u'lláh has given His followers the charge to administer the activities of their religion by the democratically elected institutions of Spiritual Assemblies and the practice of consultation. Spiritually mature people, guided by the Bahá'í principle of the organic oneness of humanity and the other teachings that support it, are encouraged to come together in consultation and create plans and programs for their material progress. Their National Spiritual Assemblies, the House of Justice (through the Office of Social and Economic Development), the Bahá'í institutions of the learned (the Continental Counselors and Auxiliary Boards), as well as other secular and governmental institutions, may all be called on for advice and assistance, but the ownership of the programs remains at the local level. This is the ninth distinctive Bahá'í practice: material development is spiritually based and can be created at the grassroots level when individuals come together in consultation.

Bahá'í activities aimed at material advancement began long before the Office for Social and Economic Development, particularly in the area of education, which is given great weight in the Bahá'í writings. Under the constant guidance and encouragement of 'Abdu'l-Bahá, and later Shoghi Effendi, the Bahá'ís of Iran were able to shake off the lethargy that permeated their nation, and using the Bahá'í formula of material development upon a spiritual foundation, became noted for their educational accomplishments. By 1973 this community had attained a 100 percent literacy rate among women under forty, compared to national literacy rate for women of less than 20 percent. After the Islamic Revolution of 1979, which closed the doors of educational opportunity for Bahá'ís in Iran, they continued to pursue educational activities through the college level, at high risk to their personal safety, with an underground system of informal schools. In other countries, Bahá'í schools, rural development projects, and educational radio stations operated and assisted both Bahá'ís and others to become self-reliant.

The Office for Social and Economic Development classifies development activities by their level of complexity. Category 1 is projects of fixed duration, which may include such things as health camps, workshops, short-term training courses and simple environmental projects. In 2005–6 there were several thousand projects of this kind initiated by Bahá'ís, mainly in third world countries. Category 2 are sustained projects, and consist of ongoing schools and services such as literacy, health care and immunization, agriculture, and microenterprise. There are about six hundred of these projects. The third type are advanced projects, which are organizations with the capacity to undertake complex actions, work in several fields simultaneously, or have the capacity to make a significant impact on the wider community. There are forty-five of these projects at present.[5]

The House of Justice recognizes that progress on issues of development is not simple, nor is one local solution always adaptable to another place. But the knowledge gained both by trial and success in one place and trial and failure in another is also valuable; one of the functions of the Office for Social and Economic Development is to serve as a clearinghouse for what has been learned thus far. The Bahá'í community, as will be explored in chapter 15, is engaged in a learning paradigm, endeavoring to discover what Bahá'u'lláh meant by a new global society, and how to create it. Mistakes are expected and welcome. The process of consultation assures Bahá'ís that, with unity, any errors will be corrected.

Along with the direct positive effects of any development project, there are also the indirect effects of capacity building within the Bahá'í community and the Spiritual Assembly. The House of Justice advises communities to start with simple, direct projects that address a single issue, and then gradually expand the scope and complexity of the projects with experience.

These development projects are tied to the Bahá'í teachings at the level of planning and evaluation through consultation, but also at the level of goals and objectives. All these projects are grounded in the central concern of establishing the oneness of humanity. Besides working on problems directly related to unity, such as the elimination of prejudice and the status of women, many of these projects also work to reinforce social teachings including the high station of service, the need for trustworthiness, sincerity, and self-sacrifice. The Bahá'í development paradigm sees man first as a spiritual being, requiring spiritual development and nourishment. Only after a sound spiritual base is built can lasting and meaningful material development take place. In the beginning, many of these projects are intended primarily for Bahá'ís, and only after they are well established are they gradually opened to the larger community.

Examples of Development Projects

To give the reader a better idea of the content of Bahá'í projects of social and economic development, here are three projects included in the 2001 booklet *For the Betterment of the World: The Worldwide Bahá'í Community's Approach to Social and Economic Development.* They illustrate the way these projects combine the spiritual and material dimensions of development. First is an example of a project of short duration, a category 1 project:

Consider, for example, a small group in Tanzania who gathered to study materials on the purpose of life, the spiritual nature of humanity, and the power of communion with God. Animated by their ongoing discussions, they broadened their collective efforts in a simple yet natural way, first to include literacy activities to better comprehend the material under study and then to address vocational needs through tailoring classes. Most of the members of the group have limited formal education. Now they testify to having acquired a strong sense of identity and to having attained new understanding and capacities. They feel galvanized by a desire to serve their communities. They have learned "how to study" and know "how to use their minds." Their neighbors "look up to them" and "recognize them as people of capacity."[6]

Here is a category 2 project that is sustained and single-faceted:

The evolution of one project, an academic school in Panama, provides a helpful example. When it opened in 1993 in a small rented house on the outskirts of Panama City, the school had three teachers and a handful of students enrolled in prekindergarten, kindergarten, and first grade. At the outset, the focus was on gaining support of the local community and establishing academic and administrative structures. Each year two or three grades were added, and eventually permanent facilities were acquired. With time, elements incorporated into the curriculum were able to infuse the learning atmosphere with such principles as the oneness of humankind, the equality of men and women, and the harmony of science and religion. Today the school offers a complete elementary education and has an ongoing teacher-training program to maintain the standard of excellence it has achieved. To strengthen family unity and promote parental involvement, it holds regular meetings for students' parents. As a service to the community, it has opened its computer laboratory as a vocational center for local women.[7]

And here is a category 3 project, which is both sustained and multifaceted:

The seed of one such organization, for example, was planted when two doctors and their families decided to move to a remote region in Honduras and do what they could to help the progress of the indigenous population. To support themselves and provide a service to the wider community, the families established a small hospital with modest surgical facilities. From this simple beginning sprang a range of programs in such areas as health education and sanitation. After a decade of activity, a nongovernmental organization then was created to give formal structure to the programs offered in the region. Emphasis shifted to the larger problems of education, and a pilot project was launched to introduce a tutorial secondary program into local communities. With support from various agencies—the Kellogg Foundation, the Department for International Development of the United Kingdom, and the Canadian International Development Agency—the organization successfully tackled the usual problems of implementation. Gradually student enrollment increased. The program has since been formally recognized by the government, and upon completing it, the students receive a fully accredited secondary diploma. The organization is now working to expand the program to other parts of the country.[8]

Many times the impetus for development projects will not come from elected institutions, but from individuals and informal groups, like these two doctors, who recognized a need and, after consultation, planned an action to address it. It may be carried out under the direct guidance of a Spiritual Assembly, or it may operate independently. But no matter how the projects are organized, the House of Justice states that all Bahá'ís have a responsibility to participate in this work: "Ultimately, the call to action is addressed to the individual friends, whether they be adult or youth, veteran or newly-enrolled. Let them step forth to take their places in the arena of service where their talents and skills, their specialized training, their material resources, their offers of time and energy and, above all, their dedication to Bahá'í principles, can be put to work in improving the lot of man."[9]

Projects in the Developed World

It is natural that Bahá'ís in developed countries will have a desire to assist in the projects in the third world. Occasionally there are opportunities to do so, but most projects are conceived on the local level and designed to be implemented by local believers, and to involve outsiders, no matter how skilled, will be difficult. In addition, it may deprive the local participants of much of the long-term learning and capacity-building benefits of the project. As more projects reach advanced stages of complexity, the opportunities for talented Bahá'ís from the developed countries will certainly multiply.

In the meantime, it is usually better for people to seek out, or start, a project in their own community. Spiritual needs are just as acute in rich societies as in poor ones. While there are many places in the United States that are in need of material development projects to create self sufficiency, there is a much more widespread need for moral education.

A moral development project in which Bahá'ís have been integrally involved, both in creation and execution, is the Virtues Project. Although founded by Bahá'ís and based on Bahá'í principles and teachings, this project is not connected with the Faith in any formal way, nor does it promote or emphasize one religion over another. The Virtues Project was founded in 1991 by three individuals who made a commitment to take action to address the rising tide of violence among families and youth. They identified 360 virtues, or qualities of character, that are found in the sacred traditions and scriptures of the world's religions and, unlike values, are independent of culture. Examples of these virtues are courage, honor, love, truthfulness, and justice. The goal of the Virtues Project is to help and inspire people to practice virtues in their everyday lives. Using trained facilitators, they offer a variety of programs to children and youth, families, and social, religious and governmental organizations. The Virtues Project materials have been translated into many languages and adopted worldwide.

The booklet *In Service to the Common Good: The American Bahá'í Community's Commitment to Social Change*, published in 2004 by the U.S. National Spiritual Assembly, profiles seven other projects and provides more in-depth case studies of four more. These range from legal assistance for abused women in the third world (the Tahirih Justice Center) to local initiatives such as Parent University (the synopsis below is paraphrased from that publication, pages 28–29).

Parent University was born from the idea of a single Bahá'í, Michael O'Neal, in response to the racial distrust and prejudice that was tearing the Savannah, Georgia, school system apart. Formally established in 2000 as a volunteer, nonprofit organization bridging the community with schools and industry organizations, the university's objectives are fourfold: to maximize student learning, to enable parents to teach one another, to involve the family in the learning process, and to provide nurturing support and guidance so families can realize their own success. It offers a broad range of courses on building successful families and communities, with an emphasis on widening the basis for children's education.

In just a few years, nearly a thousand adults have participated in programs, and it has made a significant impact on the community. In a 2003 interview, Mr. O'Neal said, "I think you'll find a different attitude among these parents toward schools. . . . Schools were once enemy territory where they entered only when their kids were in trouble. Not anymore. They're committed to their children's education."

It should come as no surprise that children and youth are a central focus of many SED projects. In 2005 the U.S. National Spiritual Assembly undertook a survey of projects by and for youth being undertaken around the country. A selection of these are described in *In Service to the Common Good: Bahá'í Youth in Their Own Words* (2005). One of the projects highlighted was the Media Training Pilot undertaken by the Native American Bahá'í Institute (NABI) in Houck, Arizona. This project trained young people from the nearby Navajo reservation to research and then conduct film interviews with two renowned Navajo artists: painter/sculptor/jewelry maker Chester Kahn and musician Knifewing Segura. Through this hands-on learning experience, the young people involved acquired new skills and self-confidence, made deeper connections with their community, and created a product that is viewed with pride by their families and community elders.

Requirements for Global Prosperity

The Bahá'í International Community prepared a document for presentation at the March 1995 World Summit for Social Development in Copenhagen titled *The Prosperity of Humankind.* It explores the spiritual basis for the concept of global prosperity and identifies six prerequisites for prosperity: consciousness of the organic oneness of humankind, the necessity for justice in human relationships, true consultation among people, universal education, instilling economic systems with spiritual values, and good governance based on democratic principles. Everyone interested in the solution of the world's problems should study this document. This chapter will close with two paragraphs from this paper, which again express the basic premise that material prosperity must be built on a spiritual foundation:

> As the twentieth century draws to a close, it is no longer possible to maintain the belief that the approach to social and economic development to which the materialistic conception of life has given rise is capable of meeting humanity's needs. Optimistic forecasts about the changes it would generate have vanished into the ever-widening abyss that separates the living standards of a small and relatively diminishing minority of the world's inhabitants from the poverty experienced by the vast majority of the globe's population.
>
> This unprecedented economic crisis, together with the social breakdown it has helped to engender, reflects a profound error of conception about human nature itself. For the levels of response elicited from human beings by the incentives of the prevailing order are not only inadequate, but seem almost irrelevant in the face of world events. We are being shown that, unless the development of society finds a purpose beyond the mere amelioration of material conditions, it will fail at attaining even these goals. That purpose must be sought in spiritual dimensions of life and motivation that transcend a constantly changing economic landscape and an artificially imposed division of human societies into "developed" and "developing."[10]

14

America and the Bahá'í Faith

From its earliest days, the Bahá'í teachings have predicted a special role for the United States as a nation and the North American (U.S. and Canadian) Bahá'í community.

A Glorious Future Predicted

Bahá'u'lláh noted how Christianity started in the East, but received its greatest development in the West. He predicted a similar future for His religion: "Say: In the East the light of His Revelation hath broken; in the West have appeared the signs of His dominion."[1]

As soon as he was released from restriction by the overthrow of the Ottoman government in 1908, 'Abdu'l-Bahá turned his attention to the West, and to America in particular. He sent emissaries to the embryonic American community, began to receive Western visitors and pilgrims, and, despite his advanced age, and health impaired from over fifty years of imprisonment and isolation, he planned for an extensive teaching trip to Europe and America that began in 1911 and was to last almost a year. Even though he had never before spoken in front of an audience, he addressed hundreds of gatherings in over forty cities in North America and nineteen more in Europe, often more than one a day, and met with hundreds more individuals and small groups. During and after this trip, he gave high praise to the American people for their energy, intelligence, spirit of openness, and enterprise, while pleading with them to abandon their materialism and racist attitudes. He also praised the American Bahá'í community, which at that juncture was functioning with no knowledge of the administrative order and only a smattering of the sacred writings translated into English. It would be fair to say that 'Abdu'l-Bahá raised up the American Bahá'í community with his own hands and feet.

In the Tablets of the Divine Plan (see chapter 15), 'Abdu'l-Bahá predicted that "the continent of America is, in the eyes of the one true God, the land wherein the splendors of His light shall be revealed, where the mysteries of His Faith shall be unveiled, where the righteous will abide and the free assemble."[2]

By spreading Bahá'u'lláh's teachings around the world, the Bahá'í community would be blessed: "The moment this divine Message is carried forward by the American believers from the shores of America and is propagated through the continents of Europe, of Asia, of Africa and of Australasia, and as far as the islands of the Pacific, this community will find itself securely established upon the throne of an everlasting dominion. Then will all the peoples of the world witness that this community is spiritually illumined and divinely guided."[3]

It was noted in chapter 7 that 'Abdu'l-Bahá took a special interest in the plight of African-American people and the state of race relations in America, reminding Americans that his father compared the African race to "the pupil of the eye" through which the spirit shines forth. In these letters he also singles out Native Americans for special prophecies, and directed the American Bahá'ís, then predominantly white and middle class, to reach out to these marginalized and impoverished groups. He assures them that native peoples, who by the beginning of the last century had been systematically stripped of their land, language, culture, and religion, have the potential to lead the entire world spiritually.*

In the decades following 'Abdu'l-Bahá's death in 1921, Shoghi Effendi addressed several lengthy letters to the American believers in which he praises the many achievements both of their nation and their community, and predicts even greater accomplishments. The American nation, he forecast, was to become central to the unfoldment of world peace. Despite being geographically remote from the perennial political trouble spots of Europe and the Middle East, the technologies of war, commerce, and communication will continue to shrink the world, so that the United States is certain to be drawn into any regional conflict. Although it initially adopted an isolationist stance, this is exactly what happened in World Wars I and II. To its credit, at the close of these exhausting conflicts, the United States did not immediately retreat into isolationism, but stepped forward and tried to create the mechanisms of world cooperation. The first of these, the League of Nations, did not have the powers needed to be effective, but the United Nations has certainly been and will continue to be a potent

---

* My understanding of the traditional religions of many Native American nations is that they comprehend the wholeness and unity of all beings and the natural world. Perhaps their "eye of oneness" is already highly developed, and this is why these people have such great potential for leadership in this day.

mechanism for peace, conflict resolution, and progress on many fronts.

Writing in 1954, Shoghi Effendi makes it clear that the future glory of the American nation will be manifest only after it abandons its outdated notions of absolute national sovereignty:

The American nation, of which the community of the Most Great Name [the Bahá'ís] forms as yet a negligible and infinitesimal part, stands, indeed, from whichever angle one observes its immediate fortunes, in grave peril. The woes and tribulations which threaten it are partly avoidable, but mostly inevitable and God-sent, for by reason of them a government and people clinging tenaciously to the obsolescent doctrine of absolute sovereignty and upholding a political system, manifestly at variance with the needs of a world already contracted into a neighborhood and crying out for unity, will find itself purged of its anachronistic conceptions, and prepared to play a preponderating role, as foretold by 'Abdu'l-Bahá, in the hoisting of the standard of the Lesser Peace, in the unification of mankind, and in the establishment of a world federal government on this planet.*

---

* Shoghi Effendi, *Citadel of Faith,* p. 126. The "Lesser Peace" is peace based on practical, political necessity. This term is used in contrast to the "Most Great Peace" which is peace based on the recognition of the organic oneness of humanity. In the light of these remarks, I find it interesting (and frightening) to watch the United States alternately take the lead in the process of building an international order, then pull back and try to abandon what it has built.

Foremost among the roles Shoghi Effendi predicted for the American Bahá'í community was to become "the cradle of the World Order of Bahá'u'lláh."[4] As previously explained, the decision-making institutions of the Bahá'í Faith are regarded as much more than practical tools for effective administration. They are, to the Bahá'ís, the central nervous system of the organic world civilization being built on Bahá'u'lláh's teachings, and, in the long term, a model for institutions of the future. To be the cradle of this administrative order is to be the place where the new global society will evolve.

A Dark Present

Why is the American nation so blessed in the Bahá'í writings, and destined to achieve such greatness? Shoghi Effendi, in *The Advent of Divine Justice,* makes it clear that this is not because of its worthiness. This passage is worth a careful reading:

> Let not, therefore, those who are to participate so predominantly in the birth of that world civilization, which is the direct offspring of their Faith [the American Bahá'í community], imagine for a moment that for some mysterious purpose or by any reason of inherent excellence or special merit Bahá'u'lláh has chosen to confer upon their country and people so great and lasting a distinction. It is precisely by reason of the patent evils which, notwithstanding its other admittedly great characteristics and achievements, an excessive and binding materialism has unfortunately engendered within it that the Author of their Faith [Bahá'u'lláh] and the Center of His Covenant ['Abdu'l-Bahá]

have singled it out to become the standard-bearer of the New World Order envisaged in their writings. It is by such means as this that Bahá'u'lláh can best demonstrate to a heedless generation His almighty power to raise up from the very midst of a people, immersed in a sea of material-ism, a prey to one of the most virulent and long-standing forms of racial prejudice, and notorious for its political corruption, lawlessness and laxity in moral standards, men and women who, as time goes by, will increasingly exem-plify those essential virtues of self-renunciation, of moral rectitude, of chastity, of indiscriminating fellowship, of holy discipline, and of spiritual insight that will fit them for the preponderating share they will have in calling into being that World Order and that World Civilization of which their country, no less than the entire human race, stands in desperate need.[5]

Bahá'u'lláh teaches that God sends His Manifestations to appear among the most spiritually dormant peoples, in order to spotlight His regenerating power. He chose to send the Báb and Bahá'u'lláh to Persia because it was among the most corrupt, superstitious, and fanatical nations on earth. In less than a century, the Iranian Bahá'í community, de-spite wave after wave of repression and persecution, became distinguished for its moral courage, incorruptibility, educa-tional attainments, emancipation of its women, and pro-gressive thought. In a parallel process, He has chosen to make America the birthplace of His new, global, spiritually based civilization because of the great evils that lie within it. The quotation above lists five of these evils: excessive and binding materialism, virulent and long-standing racial prejudice, political corruption, lawlessness, and laxity in moral standards. In the subsequent paragraphs of this letter, Shoghi Effendi examines these ills and what Bahá'ís can do to overcome them. Most Americans would not have to read too far into this document to become unsettled by the contrast between the high standards set by Bahá'u'lláh's teachings and the compromises we accept in our society.

This is the tenth distinctive practice of the Bahá'ís: They are working to make America the birthplace of a new, spiritually rich global civilization precisely because America is the last place you would expect it to happen. The American Bahá'í community continues to strive to build a system that takes the best of the American spirit while rejecting those attitudes and behaviors that are incompatible with God's new plan for the world.

Immersed in a Sea of Materialism

The evil of racial prejudice was discussed in chapter 7 and the moral standards of the Bahá'ís in chapter 4. The next several paragraphs will explore the Bahá'í teachings on materialism. What follows relies heavily on *Century of Light*, a document prepared under the supervision of the Universal House of Justice and published in 2001 as an analysis of the development of the Bahá'í Faith during the twentieth century.

At the most fundamental level, as mentioned in chapter 2, materialism maintains there is no reality beyond what can be discovered by the five senses. It dismisses the notion of a human soul and a God or other spiritual reality that has any relevance for ordinary life. Although materialism seems to have become the de facto religion of America, most Americans probably have not thought deeply about it. They slip into it by default, and it becomes for them a comfortable way of relating to life. As one early Bahá'í expressed it, they have fallen in love with their chains.

At the level of the individual, materialism sucks the spiritual out of man:

> Whether as world-view or simple appetite, materialism's effect is to leach out of human motivation—and even interest—the spiritual impulses that distinguish the rational soul. . . . In the absence of conviction about the spiritual nature of reality and the fulfillment it alone offers, it is not surprising to find at the very heart of the current crisis of civilization a cult of individualism that increasingly admits of no restraint and that elevates acquisition and personal advancement to the status of major cultural values. The resulting atomization of society has marked a new stage in the process of disintegration about which the writings of Shoghi Effendi speak so urgently.[6]

Collectively, powerful materialistic societies do the same to others. The geopolitics of the last half of the twentieth century was dominated by the struggle between two materialist ideologies: capitalism and Communism. It should be no surprise that materialism won. In the process, it destroyed much of the third world, under the guise of "assistance":

As outside forces manipulated new governments, attention was increasingly diverted from an objective consideration of developmental needs to ideological and political struggles that bore little or no relation to social or economic reality. The results were uniformly devastating. Economic bankruptcy, gross violations of human rights, the breakdown of civil administration and the rise of opportunistic elites who saw in the suffering of their countries only openings for self-enrichment—such was the heartbreaking fate that engulfed one after another of the new nations who, only short years before, had begun life with such great promise.[7]

Materialistic attitudes toward life relegate and confine religion to narrow and impotent roles of ritual, ceremony, and comfort for the distressed. It is reduced to being a pseudo-spiritual yes-man for materialism; if it finds an independent voice at all, it often lashes out as mindless protest, rage, or fanaticism: "Religion, where not simply driven back into fanaticism and unthinking rejection of progress, became progressively reduced to a kind of personal preference, a predilection, a pursuit designed to satisfy spiritual and emotional needs of the individual. The sense of historical mission that had defined the major Faiths learned to content itself with providing religious endorsement for campaigns of social change carried on by secular movements."[8] The mission of Bahá'u'lláh is to liberate all men from the bondage of materialism, racism, and nationalism so that they may build a just and peaceful world. He seeks to reestablish religion as the guiding compass in man's collective life. He wants people everywhere to be empowered with the tools of spiritual growth and collective action. He desires "the unification of humankind under a system of governance that can release the full potentialities latent in human nature, and allow their expression in programs for the benefit of all."[9] All this, Bahá'u'lláh promises, is now within humanity's reach and will come to pass as God's plan unfolds.

The False God of Freedom

A close ally of materialism and another of the false gods of American society is *freedom;* it is hard to find anyone who will speak a cautious word about it. Bahá'u'lláh's teachings are not against freedom, just as they are not against material well-being. Freedom is essential to human life; freedom of thought, expression and action are necessary for society to progress. He writes, "The Ancient Beauty [Bahá'u'lláh] hath consented to be bound with chains that mankind may be released from its bondage, and hath accepted to be made a prisoner within this most mighty Stronghold that the whole world may attain unto true liberty."[10]

Bahá'u'lláh comments extensively on freedom; on when it is beneficial to man and when it is detrimental: "We approve of liberty in certain circumstances and refuse to sanction it in others." Bahá'ís have no liberty to engage in contention or conflict, nor to foment dissension, sedition, or strife. Freedom should not be used to seek advantage or advancement over another; that is the origin of many of our problems. Bahá'u'lláh warns, "Ever since the seeking of preference and distinction came into play, the world has been laid to waste. It has become desolate. . . . Indeed, man is noble, inasmuch as each one is a repository of the sign of God. Nevertheless, to regard oneself as superior in knowledge, learning or virtue, or to exalt oneself or seek preference is a grievous transgression."[11]

Bahá'u'lláh was imprisoned for forty years for bringing a message of unity through love and justice. Unity, as discussed in chapter 3, requires agreement around a collective decision-making process and conformity with its decisions. Society should be able to expect that mature people will abide by and support the decisions that are made, whether they agree with each and every one of them or not. Shoghi Effendi explains, "The Bahá'í conception of social life is essentially based on the subordination of the individual will to that of society. It neither suppresses the individual nor does it exalt him to the point of making him an anti-social creature, a menace to society. As in everything, it follows the 'golden mean.'"[12]

The view that freedom is always good, and more freedom always better, seems to be ingrained within American culture and, along with materialism, is one of our major exports. Perhaps it is because so many peoples have struggled against unjust and oppressive governments and systems that they believe all systems are by definition unjust and oppressive. Or perhaps it is just a lack of maturity that prevents people from seeing the connection between their individual acts and the good of society. In either case, Bahá'ís are warned not to judge God's teachings with the ever-changing standards of popular culture. For them, it becomes a matter of firmness in the Covenant. Bahá'u'lláh has given guidance on the ideal method of collective decision-making (consultation), the democratic institutions to carry it out (the administrative order) and the reason for obedience to it (unity, peace, justice, and well-being). It is the obligation of the Bahá'ís, under Bahá'u'lláh's Covenant, to participate in the system that He has given them.

Unlike their Iranian brethren, who face violence and hatred from a foe with a face and name, the American Bahá'í community, if it is to achieve its destiny as the birthplace of Bahá'u'lláh's global society, must face a very different adversary. It must overcome the smothering blanket of materialism and the false god of unbounded freedom. Material society looks with suspicion on anyone who makes their faith the centerpiece of their life, and with alarm when a whole community of people does so. It bombards children and adults with the message that material comfort and pleasure are the highest goals and they are to be achieved by self-promotion, accumulation, and consumption. It shrugs its shoulders at the problems of racism, persistent extremes of wealth and poverty, and the degradation and objectification of women and says, in effect, "That's just the way it is." As long as our comfort is not threatened, it pays no serious attention to the suffering of people in other lands. Material society equates work with money, ego and prestige, not with service. Gossip, backbiting, ridicule, mistrust, disrespect, and a confrontational attitude are regarded as the natural expressions of individual freedom, the path to social advancement, the primary method of politics, and the mainstay of entertainment. Decisions are made by those with power, and "follow the money" is too-often the path to truth. The American Bahá'ís have their work cut out for them.

15

It's Systematic *and* Spiritual

Bahá'u'lláh's revelation, He teaches, has created new spiritual capacities that make possible the unification of all peoples in a just global society and true peace among nations. But these capacities are latent. They require people who will rise up and take the steps necessary to develop and release this capacity in themselves or others. These people are Bahá'u'lláh's new race of men. Since its earliest days, the Bahá'í Faith has adopted a systematic strategy to find these people.

The Worldwide Expansion of the Bahá'í Religion

For many, the notion that a person, action, practice or institution is spiritual implies that it cannot be systematic. All spiritual things are, to them, spontaneous, random, inspired or unpredictable. The eleventh distinctive practice of the Bahá'ís is this: Not only *can* spiritual things be approached systematically, many spiritual things *must be.* The spiritually mature person will be systematic in his approach to his relationship with God. He will study the sacred texts regularly, pray, and contribute materially to his faith. The new society that Bahá'u'lláh wants can only be achieved when the rank and file of people grow in maturity, come together in consultation, and take action for the benefit of all. To accomplish its mission, the leaders of the Bahá'í Faith (as specified in the Covenant), have all created systematic plans with clear objectives and measurable goals. The Bahá'ís regard these plans as an integral part of their religion.*

During the darkest days of World War I, when Palestine was effectively cut off from the rest of the world and the Bahá'ís in Acre, along with the other residents, suffered from extreme deprivation, 'Abdu'l-Bahá mapped out a plan for the spread of the Faith throughout the world. The Tablets of the Divine Plan, as these fourteen letters are known, were addressed to the Bahá'ís of North America and laid upon them the primary responsibility for the spread of the Bahá'í teachings. These letters, which could not even be delivered until the end of the war, still form the spiritual foundation on which Bahá'í plans are developed.

The Divine Plan of 'Abdu'l-Bahá immediately inspired a number of American believers, primarily women, to forsake their homes and travel to the then-remote corners of Africa, Asia, Latin America, and the Pacific to establish Bahá'í communities. Then as now, individual initiative was critical to successfully meeting the goals of a plan. But other aspects of 'Abdu'l-Bahá's plan required further development of the administrative institutions and action at a collective level. Shoghi Effendi devoted the first years of his tenure as Guardian to directing the Bahá'ís to form effective institutions at the local

---

* Of course, it is possible to move too far toward systematization, where religion degenerates into a rigid and mindless repetition of prayers, rituals and recitations, and fund-raising activities. Bahá'u'lláh quotes the Islamic tradition that "One hour's reflection is preferable to seventy years of pious worship." (Kitáb-i-Íqán, ¶269.) He gives His followers the freedom to engage their minds in spiritual pursuits, and He expects them to do so. While systematic plans are an essential component of His religion, each individual Bahá'í must ultimately decide how he can best support them.

and national levels. Once these were in place, he developed the first Seven Year Plan (1937–44), that had as its goals the establishment of at least one Local Spiritual Assembly in every state and province of North America, the development of communities in every country of Latin America, and the completion of the exterior ornamentation of the House of Worship in Wilmette, Illinois. This was followed by the second Seven Year Plan (1946–53), which continued the spread of the Faith to more countries and lands, especially in Latin America and Africa, and then by the Ten Year Crusade (1953–63), resulting in the election of the first Universal House of Justice by the fifty-four National Spiritual Assemblies on the anniversary of Bahá'u'lláh's public announcement in Baghdad one hundred years before. During that century, the Bahá'í Faith grew from a single obscure prisoner of the Ottoman Empire to a worldwide religion.

An Outward-Looking Community

Under the guidance of the Universal House of Justice, further plans were created for the expansion of the Faith of Bahá'u'lláh. These plans were similar to the earlier plans of Shoghi Effendi: they called for Bahá'ís to arise and serve as pioneers and travel teachers to specific destinations, for National and Local Assemblies to be formed, for Houses of Worship, Bahá'í schools, and other properties to be developed, and for the sacred writings and other literature to be translated into more languages. Then in 1996, the House of Justice released a plan for the Bahá'í world, the Four Year Plan, that signaled a new direction in the global development of the Faith. This new plan, the Five Year Plan that followed (2001–6), and the Five Year Plan announced in 2006 created an exciting new vision for Bahá'í communities. Many Bahá'ís, including this writer, are still laboring to fully comprehend the significance and scope of this vision. The rest of this chapter is my understanding of what Bahá'ís today are being asked to do.

The primary goal of the first eighty years of plans, to spread the Bahá'í religion to the entire globe, has largely been attained. It is the second-most widespread of the world's religions, after Christianity. At the time of this writing (2007), there are Bahá'í communities in 190 countries and 46 additional territories and islands, with 183 National Spiritual Assemblies and thousands of Local Spiritual Assemblies. The breadth of the worldwide Bahá'í community has been developed; the House of Justice is now asking the Bahá'ís to work on its depth. The House of Justice states large scale growth, predicted by Shoghi Effendi as "entry by troops of peoples of divers nations and races into the Bahá'í world,"[1] will happen in all countries, and for Bahá'í communities to be unprepared is a grave error.

As discussed in chapter 7, Bahá'u'lláh requires His followers to associate with people of all nations, races, and religions in a spirit of kindliness and fellowship. This instruction extends beyond mere friendship, however. It also means offering to others those teachings they may find valuable in facing challenges in their lives. Teachings such as the importance of education, the damage done by racial prejudice, the fundamental harmony of religions, consultation as an alternative to power and contention in decision-making, and the overriding need for unity among peoples are all dynamic principles that many find to be invaluable compass-points in their lives whether or not they comprehend or accept the Bahá'í message in its entirety. The new plans put forward by the House of Justice starting in 1996 ask the Bahá'ís to become more outward-looking in the application and diffusing of Bahá'u'lláh's teachings. To do this, the rank and file of Bahá'ís must become, first, better grounded in the fundamental teachings and practices of their religion, and second, more focused in their avenue of service they employ to offer these to humanity.

A New Institution and a New Method

In the Four Year Plan of 1996, the Universal House of Justice established a new institution on a worldwide scale, the *Regional Training Institute,* and made it responsible for delivering Bahá'ís both new and old the vision and education they need to carry out the new plans. The members of the Training Institutes are appointed by the National Assembly or Regional Council in each country or area. The Training Institute's primary function at present is to train tutors and facilitators who will offer carefully designed courses to Bahá'í individuals and communities. There are a wide range of courses developed in different parts of the world, for example: training for members and officers of Local Assemblies, for parents and families, and for teachers of children's classes. But the most basic educational program, designed for all Bahá'ís and anyone interested in learning about the Bahá'ís, is the study circle.

The study circle is a participatory method of basic Bahá'í education using a well-tested curriculum, a facilitator, and a group of Bahá'ís who meet on a regular basis. Initially there were several alternative study circle curricula in use, but the one produced by the Ruhi Institute, a Bahá'í educational institution headquartered in Puerta Tejada, Colombia, and operated under the guidance of the National Spiritual Assembly of Colombia, has since been adopted worldwide and endorsed by the Universal House of Justice. The nation of Colombia, despite a high level of social turmoil and violence caused by long and bloody civil and drug wars, has experienced very rapid growth in the size of its Bahá'í community. By the 1970s this growth was overwhelming the available human resources for spiritual education of the new Bahá'ís, new communities and new Spiritual Assemblies. Faced with the need for a new method to develop these resources, the Ruhi Institute was born.

The Ruhi Institute released a *Statement of Method and Purpose* [2] that describes its philosophy of education, development, and social change. Building on Bahá'u'lláh's explicit teachings, it sees the spiritual development of the individual and the development of a new society as two processes in continual interaction. Spiritual education, consisting of memorization, group study, and discussion of selected Bahá'í writings, is a central component of the study circle. But the Ruhi process goes on from this foundation, focusing on channeling individual spiritual education continuously into consultation and then into community building and social action. The social outcome of a course or program is not fixed at its outset; the participants own the process and are free to experiment with alternative services and actions. Each participant in the program, called a collaborator to emphasize his active role, acts as a student in some educational activities and a tutor in others.

The most critical point is that in the Ruhi process, education consists of both study and action going hand in hand. Its goal is to empower individuals to become strong, mature spiritual beings and catalysts for collective action. It is not enough to study and then do nothing with what you have learned.

The Core Activities

Although they are open to anyone, the Ruhi study circles are designed primarily to assist Bahá'ís in their growth and empowerment. They equip the individual with the knowledge and skills needed to arise to serve in various capacities. Four particular avenues of service have become known as the *core activities,* which the House of Justice deems essential to the outward-looking vision of the Bahá'í Faith at this time.

The first of the core activities is the study circle itself. The Ruhi study circles are arranged in a sequence. As currently practiced in the United States, there are seven, with the final one being preparation to become a tutor. Thus the process is self-replicating. This is a very important avenue of service, to become a study circle facilitator and thus assist in the development of the human resources the Bahá'í Faith needs for systematic growth.

A second avenue of service stressed in the Ruhi course sequence is to organize and offer devotional gatherings open to all. While prayers and devotions have always been part of activities such as Nineteen Day Feasts and holy day observances, the simple act of communal devotion, in which every participant is free to worship and praise God in the medium and words of his choosing, is an especially powerful means of binding the hearts and uniting the wills of ordinary people. Bahá'ís around the world are experimenting with creative ways of facilitating these gatherings. The devotionals are not formulaic or rigid, but should be dignified and respectful of the sensitivities of the participants. Since beauty is an important component of Bahá'í worship, the organizers are free to incorporate music and the visual, verbal, and performing arts as wisdom dictates.

A third avenue of service stemming from the Ruhi curricula is to offer spiritual and moral education to children. Formal children's classes are often the first educational activities developed in Bahá'í communities, but the new outward emphasis challenges them to find ways to offer educational programs to the wider community. They often find that many parents, while they may not practice any particular religion themselves, nevertheless feel a need for systematic spiritual and moral education for their children. The House of Justice says that all Bahá'í communities need to have children's education as a core activity, available to all.

Finally, in the Five Year Plan that began 2006, programs for young people ages 12–15, known as "junior youth," have been added to the list of core activities that each community must try to strengthen. Junior youth are at the threshold of the age of maturity, and require a different set of educational methods than younger children. They are more likely to learn from the example of their peers than their elders, and the

Ruhi curricula for these young people emphasizes the development of critical thinking skills and constructive action by examining the lives of other young men and women. Again, the intention is that these programs should be open not just to Bahá'ís but to the larger community.

Developing a Culture of Learning

Besides the emphasis on systematic spiritual education through study circles and the development of core activities of service open to all, there are other goals and strategies in the recent plans that also point in new directions for the Bahá'ís. One is the organization of their countries into units of planning and action called *clusters*. These are more-or-less homogeneous demographic areas with a given level of Bahá'í activity, as measured by the number of believers and the development of Spiritual Assemblies and the programs of the Training Institutes. The purpose of the cluster is not to add another layer to the Bahá'í administrative order, but simply to help Bahá'ís and their institutions assess the progress of the plans in their locality and take whatever actions are appropriate for its success.

Another constant theme of the recent plans is the importance of including the performing, visual, and verbal arts in all Bahá'í activities, whether for adults, youth, or children. Experience shows that incorporating beauty and art into any activity creates a surge of spiritual energy that uplifts and motivates the participants.

The institutions of the cluster and the Training Institute, the method of the study circle and the Ruhi curriculum, and the concept of outward-looking core activities of service are all new developments in the Bahá'í world. They are not static creations but are in a state of organic growth and development. In fact, according to the House of Justice, the entire Bahá'í community should regard itself as a culture of learning, where new approaches are developed through a recurring cycle of consultation, action, and reflection. This learning culture does not just apply to the elected institutions; it applies to all groups of Bahá'ís: families, study circles, the Nineteen Day Feast, Spiritual Assemblies, Training Institutes, and clusters. It is a natural extension of 'Abdu'l-Bahá's promise that, if decisions arrived at through consultation are carried out with unity, any mistakes will be readily identified and easily corrected.

16

To Become a Bahá'í

When a group of Bahá'ís gather, especially if they do not know each other very well, it is common for them to tell the stories of how they came to discover and embrace the Bahá'í religion. Hearing these stories will reinforce the truth that the search for religious certitude is a personal and private journey. No two stories are identical. Some people accept the Faith the first time they hear about it; others after years of independent investigation.

To become a Bahá'í is easy. The Universal House of Justice has listed the requirements for a seeker to be enrolled in the Bahá'í community. She must believe that Bahá'u'lláh is the Manifestation of God for today, accept the provisions of the Bahá'í Covenant, and agree to do her best to obey the institutions and to live according to the Bahá'í laws and teachings. If a person understands and agrees to these requirements she is admitted to the Bahá'í community and has the same rights and privileges as any other member. It is not for anyone to judge the worthiness of another.

To thrive as a Bahá'í is not always easy, however. The Universal House of Justice promises, "No one should expect, upon becoming a Bahá'í, that his faith will not be tested."[1] Tests and difficulties will come from all directions: from the society around him, his family and friends, and even his fellow Bahá'ís. But the most severe tests will almost certainly come from his own ego, which rebels against maturity, spirituality, unity, and transformation into a new being. Baháʼuʼlláh states repeatedly that trials and tests are God's tools for helping us learn and advance. His followers should regard them as signs of His love, and be assured that He will not test anyone beyond his capacity.

Being a Baháʼí means adopting some attitudes and behaviors that are at odds with what contemporary Western society sanctions. But more fundamentally, it means becoming a mature, strong, and spiritual being, with belief in God and His love, as revealed through the Manifestations, at his core. For someone coming from a culture dominated by materialism, where religion is relegated to a narrow compartment of life, this can be a huge step. It may require a great struggle before his soul is released from its bondage and given permission to develop a full relationship with God. Baháʼuʼlláh gives the formula for this transformation: detaching oneself from the world and its traditions, experiencing the words of the Manifestations, and asking God for assistance. If you are already a spiritual person you have much to be thankful for, no matter what your religious affiliation.

The House of Justice lists six basic steps that define the Baháʼí path to spirituality. These allow a believer to take ownership of his own spiritual growth and development and build a mature relationship with his Maker, one that will grow stronger with time:

Baháʼuʼlláh has stated quite clearly in His Writings the essential requisites for our spiritual growth, and these are stressed again and again by ʻAbduʼl-Bahá in His talks and Tablets. One can summarize them briefly in this way:

1. The recital each day of one of the Obligatory Prayers with pure-hearted devotion.*

2. The regular reading of the Sacred Scriptures, specifically at least each morning and evening, with reverence, attention and thought.

3. Prayerful meditation on the Teachings, so that we may understand them more deeply, fulfill them more faithfully, and convey them more accurately to others.

4. Striving every day to bring our behavior more into accordance with the high standards that are set forth in the Teachings.

5. Teaching the Cause of God.

6. Selfless service in the work of the Cause and in the carrying on of our trade and profession.[2]

For most, the process of spiritual growth will be gradual. "Little by little, day by day" is the regimen for growth attributed to 'Abdu'l-Bahá.

The Bahá'í standards for personal behavior, it should be clear by now, are very high. But they are standards, not requirements. When someone becomes a Bahá'í, he agrees to adopt these standards and strive toward them. He does not have to immediately understand or conform to all the

---

* The Kitáb-i-Aqdas contains three special prayers, called the *Obligatory Prayers*. Bahá'ís are responsible for reciting one of their choosing daily, following the requirements set forth in that book. The Short Obligatory Prayer, which can be recited any time between noon and sunset, is as follows: "I bear witness, O my God, that thou hast created me to know Thee and to worship Thee. I testify, at this moment, to my powerlessness and to Thy might, to my poverty and to Thy wealth. There is none other God but Thee, the Help in Peril, the Self-Subsisting."

teachings to be a Bahá'í. Falling short should be expected. Remember that there is no confession in the Faith, nor gossip or backbiting, so one's shortcomings remain between himself and God while he works to overcome them. If there is some aspect of belief or practice that is hard to understand, it is all right to put it aside for a time and say, "I'll try to understand this later." Every individual Bahá'í has flaws and shortcomings, but that need not prevent him from being of service to humanity.

All Bahá'ís, new and old, wish their local communities were the unified, loving, and just societies that Bahá'u'lláh wants. While each is unique and at its own stage of development, they are all far from being finished. They are embryonic. It is the job of the Bahá'ís to build them, not for themselves, but for generations to come. Great blessings, as well as tests, come from involvement in this process. This is where a believer will get to practice eliminating prejudice, avoiding gossip and backbiting, experiencing the joys of working with children and youth (or, perhaps, being a child or youth), and learning the art of consultation. This is where he will be challenged to instantly forgive everyone who wrongs him. He will be asked to serve in various ways, on programs and projects of the Spiritual Assembly; perhaps he will be elected to the Assembly itself.

For many Bahá'ís, the demands of community life are a test of maturity. On the one hand, the needs are great, and he knows that God promises compensation for sacrifices in His path; sacrifices today lay the foundation for accomplishments tomorrow. On the other, there are only so many hours in the day and there are other responsibilities and obligations. Integrating the Bahá'í work with the rest of one's life is a never-ending challenge; (dare I say it one last time?) maturity is required.

Within the Bahá'í community you will find people at all stages of spiritual development. Shoghi Effendi once wrote that someday the Bahá'ís will be "a hundred times more mature"[3] than they are now. One must always remember that she is responsible only for her own spiritual progress, not the progress of any of her fellow believers.

To thrive as a Bahá'í today is being made much easier by the new institution of the Regional Training Institute and its programs. It is a powerful resource for spiritual growth and maturity that was not available a few years ago. No longer does one have to chart his own course through the Bahá'í teachings. By all means, a new Bahá'í should avail himself of the Training Institute's programs. The study circles, especially, are places one can join with other seekers and systematically explore and practice the meaning of the Bahá'í teachings in an atmosphere of love and equality. Through them one will begin to manifest the new spiritual potentials Bahá'u'lláh's revelation has created within him.

Even using the sacred scriptures, prayers, and the resources of the Training Institutes, there may be times when it seems that one's spiritual growth has stalled. The Bahá'í standards will seem unreachable. It is important to be patient. For many, the spiritual maturity God wants will take a lifetime (or longer) to achieve. There will be years when other cares or problems make it difficult to give much of one's energy to God's work. These are part of the natural cycles of human life. If one can get through these with his faith intact, there will again be times when he can again make God's imperative central in his life. The House of Justice says that, at a minimum, all Bahá'ís can teach the Faith, pray, contribute something to the Bahá'í funds, and "fight their own spiritual battles."[4] Remember the "mystery of sacrifice": God promises to assist those who arise and struggle.

Belief in Bahá'u'lláh is the only sure foundation for being a Bahá'í. Many people are attracted to the unifying teachings of the Bahá'í Faith on a practical level: the equality of women and men, the elimination of racial prejudice, universal education, the elimination of the extremes of wealth and poverty, and the establishment of international understanding, peace, order, and justice. The world certainly needs as many people as possible committed to these goals, whether they are Bahá'ís or not.

But there is a difference between Bahá'u'lláh's followers and others with similar aims. Bahá'ís believe these other issues are all subordinate to one fundamental, God-decreed imperative: to establish a new society based on the unshakable recognition of the oneness and wholeness of humankind. This is the highest, most difficult mission to which a person can commit himself. If this truly is God's desire, then anything less is a compromise. This mandate must be approached as a spiritual, not a material, mission. This is the healing edge of religion. Only those who believe this is God's decree will have an unwavering commitment to it, humbly seeking His assistance while accepting no half-measures and remaining undeterred by obstacles. These people are the Bahá'ís.

Notes

Foreword

1. Matthew 7:29 (NIV).

Chapter 1

1. For a detailed study of biblical prophecies pointing to this time, see Michael Sours, *The Prophecies of Jesus* (Oxford: Oneworld Publications, 1991).

2. Bahá'u'lláh, *Gleanings*, no. 139. *Gleanings* is a selection of Bahá'u'lláh's writings compiled and translated by Shoghi Effendi and first published in 1939. It includes selections from the Kitáb-i-Íqán, the Kitáb-i-Aqdas, and other works.

   Of Bahá'u'lláh's vast writings, only a portion have been translated into English from the original Arabic and Farsi (Persian), but these include most of the important doctrinal works. The remainder (the largest quantity of His writings) have been characterized as primarily "advice and encouragement" that was originally addressed to specific individuals. The entire body of Bahá'u'lláh's writings, as well as those of 'Abdu'l-Bahá and Shoghi Effendi, are housed in the archives at the Bahá'í World Center on the slopes of Mount Carmel in Haifa, Israel. Careful translation of the remainder is proceeding in an orderly fashion, using those works and passages translated by Shoghi Effendi as models. It was also Shoghi Effendi who chose the system of transliteration used to translate proper names from Arabic and Farsi into English. I have followed this transliteration only for the most commonly used Bahá'í names.

   Very often the most important passages of Bahá'í scripture that I quote are published in several compilations and quoted in subsequent works. I have tried to reference the complete work when it is available, or the most accessible source when it is not.

3. Bahá'u'lláh, *Tablets of Bahá'u'lláh,* pp. 221–22. The volume *Tablets of Bahá'u'lláh* contains complete translations of several important works in which Bahá'u'lláh amplifies and explains the provisions of the Kitáb-i-Aqdas.
4. Bahá'u'lláh, quoted in Shoghi Effendi, *The World Order of Bahá-'u'lláh,* p. 135. The World Order of Bahá'u'lláh is a compilation of seven letters from Shoghi Effendi to the Bahá'ís of North America written during the period 1929–36. He used these letters to explain the broad vision of Bahá'u'lláh's teachings. Shoghi Effendi often translated and included passages from the writings of Bahá'u'lláh and 'Abdu'l-Bahá in his letters. These passages are now used as the basis for full translations.
5. 'Abdu'l-Bahá, *Will and Testament,* p. 11. The Will and Testament of 'Abdu'l-Bahá is in many ways a supplement to Bahá'u'lláh's book of laws, the Kitáb-i-Aqdas. 'Abdu'l-Bahá uses this document not only to appoint Shoghi Effendi as Guardian, but also to further explain the functioning of the elected and appointed institutions of the Bahá'í Faith (see chapter 6). As a warning to the Bahá'ís, he also recounts some of the troubles caused by the handful of Bahá'ís who had rejected Bahá'u'lláh's Covenant and tried to sabotage His mission.
6. 1 Corinthians 12:8–11 (NIV).
7. Bahá'u'lláh, *Gleanings,* no. 134.
8. 'Abdu'l-Bahá, quoted by Shoghi Effendi in *The World Order of Bahá'u'lláh,* p. 36.
9. 'Abdu'l-Bahá, *Selections from the Writings of 'Abdu'l-Bahá,* no. 192.
10. Ibid., no. 185.

Chapter 2

1. Bahá'u'lláh, *Gleanings,* no. 34.
2. Bahá'u'lláh, *Gleanings,* no. 27.
3. Koran, 30:40.
4. Bahá'u'lláh, Kitáb-i-Aqdas, 161–63.
5. Matthew 24:29 (NIV).

6. Bahá'u'lláh, Kitáb-i-Íqán, ¶41. This book was translated from Farsi into English by Shoghi Effendi in 1931.
7. Bahá'u'lláh, *Gleanings*, no. 81.
8. Bahá'u'lláh, Hidden Words, Persian, no. 3. The Hidden Words is probably Bahá'u'lláh's best-known work. It contains "the inner essence" of religion, "clothed in the garment of brevity." The first part is in Arabic, the second in Persian.
9. 2 Timothy 3:5 (NIV).
10. Matthew 7:8 (NIV).
11. Bahá'u'lláh, *Gleanings*, no. 50.
12. Bahá'u'lláh, Kitáb-i-Íqán, ¶2.
13. Ibid., ¶16–17.
14. The Báb, *Selections from the Writings of the Báb*, no. 3:2.

Chapter 3

1. Bahá'u'lláh, quoted in Shoghi Effendi, *God Passes By*, p. 217. *God Passes By* is Shoghi Effendi's detailed history of the first one hundred years of the Bábí and Bahá'í religions, 1844–1944. It is the authoritative reference for most of the historical material presented in chapter 1.
2. Shoghi Effendi, *The Promised Day Is Come*, p. 122. *The Promised Day Is Come* is a lengthy letter addressed to the Bahá'ís of the world by Shoghi Effendi in 1941, interpreting recent world history in light of Bahá'u'lláh's teachings and predictions.
3. Bahá'u'lláh, *Gleanings*, no. 131.
4. Shoghi Effendi, *The Promised Day Is Come*, p. 122.
5. Shoghi Effendi, *The World Order of Bahá'u'lláh*, p. 202.
6. The Universal House of Justice, *The Promise of World Peace*, p. 1.
7. Ibid.
8. Shoghi Effendi, *The World Order of Bahá'u'lláh*, p. 170.
9. The Universal House of Justice, *The Promise of World Peace*, p. 13.
10. Bahá'í World Center, *Century of Light*, p. 41. *Century of Light* was prepared under the guidance of the House of Justice and is an analysis of the growth and development of the Bahá'í Faith during the twentieth century. It will be quoted extensively in chapter 14.

11. Bahá'u'lláh, *Tablets of Bahá'u'lláh*, p. 66.

12. The Universal House of Justice, *Issues Related to the Study of the Bahá'í Faith*, p. 22.

Chapter 4

1. Shoghi Effendi, *The Advent of Divine Justice*, pp. 22, 30. *The Advent of Divine Justice* is a book-length letter addressed by Shoghi Effendi to the American Bahá'í community in 1938 that describes the spiritual and moral challenges they face. He devotes several paragraphs to the meaning of "rectitude of conduct" and the requirements of a "chaste and holy life." Some other topics contained in this letter are examined in later chapters.

2. Bahá'u'lláh, Kitáb-i-Íqán, ¶272.

3. Bahá'u'lláh, quoted in Shoghi Effendi, *The Advent of Divine Justice*, p. 17. Shoghi Effendi quotes Bahá'u'lláh as calling on humanity to become "a new race of men." This phrase has become widely used by Bahá'ís to describe the degree of transformation Bahá'u'lláh expects from His followers.

4. 'Abdu'l-Bahá, quoted in Shoghi Effendi, *The Promised Day Is Come*, p. 119.

5. Bahá'u'lláh, *Gleanings*, no. 36.

6. Bahá'u'lláh, *Prayers and Meditations*, pp. 295–96.

7. Bahá'u'lláh, *Gleanings*, no. 132.

8. Ibid., no. 5.

Chapter 5

1. Bahá'u'lláh, *Gleanings*, no. 27.

2. Bahá'u'lláh, *The Seven Valleys*, p. 4.

3. Bahá'u'lláh, Kitáb-i-Íqán, ¶167.

4. Bahá'u'lláh, *The Seven Valleys*, p. 5.

5. Bahá'u'lláh, Kitáb-i-Íqán, ¶1.

6. Bahá'u'lláh, *Gleanings*, no. 134.

7. 'Abdu'l-Bahá, *The Promulgation of Universal Peace*, p. 291.

8. Bahá'u'lláh, *Tablets of Bahá'u'lláh*, p. 26.

9. 'Abdu'l-Bahá, *The Promulgation of Universal Peace*, p. 49.

10. Ibid., p. 50.

11. 'Abdu'l-Bahá, *Selections From the Writings of 'Abdu'l-Bahá*, no. 205.

12. Bahá'u'lláh, *Tablets of Bahá'u'lláh*, p. 169.

13. 'Abdu'l-Bahá, *The Promulgation of Universal Peace*, p. 229.

14. 'Abdu'l-Bahá, *'Abdu'l-Bahá in London*, pp. 28–29.

15. Bahá'u'lláh, *Gleanings*, no. 99.

16. Bahá'u'lláh, *Tablets of Bahá'u'lláh*, p. 162.

17. Ibid., p. 90.

18. 'Abdu'l-Bahá, *'Abdu'l-Bahá in London*, p. 91.

Chapter 6

1. Bahá'u'lláh, Kitáb-i-Aqdas, ¶34.

2. Bahá'u'lláh, *Tablets of Bahá'u'lláh*, p. 24

3. Bahá'u'lláh, Kitáb-i-Aqdas, ¶57.

4. The Universal House of Justice, *Individual Rights and Freedoms*, p. 10. This letter from the House of Justice to the Bahá'ís of the United States concerns the balance that must be achieved in their community between individual liberty and unified action. This topic will be taken up again in chapter 14.

Chapter 7

1. Matthew 7:28 (NIV).

2. Bahá'u'lláh, *Tablets of Bahá'u'lláh*, p. 87.

3. 'Abdu'l-Bahá, *Selections from the Writings of 'Abdu'l-Bahá*, no. 202.2–3

4. The Universal House of Justice, *Messages from the Universal House of Justice*, no. 117.2.

5. Bahá'u'lláh, Hidden Words, Arabic, no. 68. I have never been able to read this particular passage without the chilling feeling that God is addressing me personally.

6. 'Abdu'l-Bahá, in *Bahá'í Prayers*, pp. 101–2. This particular prayer was first recited by 'Abdu'l-Bahá at All Souls Church in Chicago on May 5, 1912.

7. 'Abdu'l-Bahá, *Paris Talks*, no. 15.7.

8. Ibid., pp. 15–6.

9. 'Abdu'l-Bahá, quoted in Shoghi Effendi, *The Advent of Divine Justice*, p. 37.

10. Shoghi Effendi, *The Advent of Divine Justice*, pp. 28–29.

11. Ibid., p. 29.

12. Ibid., p. 33.

13. Ibid., pp. 33–4.

14. Ibid., p. 34.

15. National Spiritual Assembly of the Bahá'ís of the United States, *The Vision of Race Unity*, p. 11.

16. 'Abdu'l-Bahá, *The Promulgation of Universal Peace*, p. 375.

17. National Spiritual Assembly of the Bahá'ís of the United States, *Two Wings of a Bird*, pp. 8–9 (italics in original).

Chapter 8

1. Bahá'u'lláh, Kitáb-i-Íqán, ¶193.

2. Bahá'u'lláh, Hidden Words, Arabic, no. 27.

3. 'Abdu'l-Bahá, quoted in *Star of the West* 4, no. 11 (1913): 192. *Star of the West* was a Bahá'í magazine that often included translated talks and letters of 'Abdu'l-Bahá. It was published from 1910–24.

4. Shoghi Effendi, in "Living the Life," *The Compilation of Compilations* 2:3. "The Master" is a title given to 'Abdu'l-Bahá by his father.

5. 'Abdu'l-Bahá, *Selections from the Writings of 'Abdu'l-Bahá*, no. 35.

6. Matthew 7:1–5 (NIV).

7. Bahá'u'lláh, *Gleanings*, no. 145. God conceals our faults as a mercy to us, not because of our merit. See for example, Bahá'u'lláh, Hidden Words, Persian, no. 60.

8. 'Abdu'l-Bahá, *Selections from the Writings of 'Abdu'l-Bahá*, no. 193.

9. Ibid., no. 144.

10. 'Abdu'l-Bahá, quoted in *Star of the West* 8, no. 11 (1917): 138.
11. Shoghi Effendi, included in *Lights of Guidance,* no. 325.
12. 'Abdu'l-Bahá, *The Promulgation of Universal Peace,* p. 453.

Chapter 9

1. Bahá'u'lláh, *Tablets of Bahá'u'lláh,* p. 168.
2. Bahá'u'lláh, in *Spiritual Assemblies and Bahá'í Consultation,* p. 79.
3. 'Abdu'l-Bahá, quoted in *Lights of Guidance,* no. 580.
4. 'Abdu'l-Bahá, quoted in *Star of the West* 8, no. 9 (1917): 114.
5. The Universal House of Justice, *Lights of Guidance,* no. 590.
6. 'Abdu'l-Bahá, quoted in the Universal House of Justice, *Individual Rights and Freedoms,* pp. 13–14.
7. 'Abdu'l-Bahá, quoted in *Star of the West* 6, no. 6 (1915): 45.
8. Shoghi Effendi, quoted in *Lights of Guidance,* no. 151.
9. Shoghi Effendi, *Bahá'í Administration,* pp. 63–64. *Bahá'í Administration* is a collection of excerpts from Shoghi Effendi's letters concerning administrative topics.
10. Bahá'u'lláh, quoted in *Spiritual Assemblies and Bahá'í Consultation,* p. 79.
11. 'Abdu'l-Bahá, *Selections from the Writings of 'Abdu'l-Bahá,* no. 43.
12. Shoghi Effendi, *Bahá'í Administration,* p. 88.

Chapter 10

1. 'Abdu'l-Bahá, *Will and Testament,* p. 15.
2. 'Abdu'l-Bahá, *Paris Talks,* no 49.9–12.
3. Shoghi Effendi, *Directives from the Guardian,* p. 56.
4. Ibid.
5. From a letter written on behalf of the Universal House of Justice, January 12, 2003, to an individual Bahá'í.

Chapter 11

1. Matthew 23:11 (NIV).
2. Bahá'u'lláh, *Tablets of Bahá'u'lláh,* p. 138.

3. 'Abdu'l-Bahá, quoted in Shoghi Effendi, *The World Order of Bahá'u'lláh,* p. 139.

4. The Universal House of Justice, *To the World's Religious Leaders,* p. 5. This open letter, addressed to the leaders of all the world's religions, calls on them not only to not resist the forces uniting the world, but to lead them.

5. Bahá'u'lláh, Kitáb-i-Aqdas, ¶33.

6. Bahá'u'lláh, Hidden Words, Persian, no. 54.

7. Ibid., no. 53.

8. Bahá'u'lláh, *Gleanings,* no. 128.

9. Bahá'u'lláh, *Tablets of Bahá'u'lláh,* p. 71.

10. Bahá'u'lláh, Hidden Words, Persian, no. 49.

11. Bahá'u'lláh, *Gleanings,* no. 145.

12. Bahá'u'lláh, in Ḥuqúqu'lláh, p. 2.

Chapter 12

1. Nabíl-i-A'ẓam, *The Dawn-Breakers,* p. 94. *The Dawn-Breakers* is a detailed eyewitness account of the tumultuous first years of the Bábí and Bahá'í religions. Written by Nabíl-i-A'ẓam and edited and translated into English by Shoghi Effendi, it is often studied by Bahá'í youth in their classes and summer schools.

2. The Universal House of Justice, *Messages from the Universal House of Justice,* no. 37.5.

3. Bahá'í World Center, *Century of Light,* p. 101.

4. The Universal House of Justice, *Youth,* pp. 118–19.

5. 'Abdu'l-Bahá, *Selections from the Writings of 'Abdu'l-Bahá,* no. 114.

6. Ibid., no. 110.2.

Chapter 13

1. Bahá'u'lláh, *Gleanings,* no. 106.

2. 'Abdu'l-Bahá, *The Secret of Divine Civilization,* pp. 12–13.

3. The Universal House of Justice, *Readings on Bahá'í Social and Economic Development,* p. 4.

4. Ibid., p. 5.
5. Bahá'í International Community, *The Bahá'í World 2005–2006,* pp. 251–52.
6. Bahá'í International Community, *For the Betterment of the World,* p. 9.
7. Ibid., p. 13.
8. Ibid., p. 21.
9. The Universal House of Justice, *Readings on Bahá'í Social and Economic Development,* p. 6.
10. Bahá'í International Community, *The Prosperity of Humankind,* p. 3.

Chapter 14

1. Bahá'u'lláh, *Tablets of Bahá'u'lláh,* p. 13.
2. 'Abdu'l-Bahá, *Tablets of the Divine Plan,* p. 62.
3. Ibid., p. 40.
4. Shoghi Effendi, *The Advent of Divine Justice,* p. 19.
5. Ibid., p. 16.
6. Bahá'í World Center, *Century of Light,* pp. 89–90. The "rational soul" is a term used by 'Abdu'l-Bahá which is roughly synonymous with "the mind," in the highest sense of the word.
7. The Universal House of Justice, *Century of Light,* pp. 88–89.
8. Ibid., p. 89.
9. Ibid., p. 91.
10. Bahá'u'lláh, *Gleanings,* no. 45.
11. Ibid., no. 159; Bahá'u'lláh, quoted in *Messages from the Universal House of Justice,* no. 206.3a.
12. Shoghi Effendi, *Directives from the Guardian,* p. 53.

Chapter 15

1. Shoghi Effendi, *Citadel of Faith,* p. 117.
2. The Universal House of Justice, in *Readings on Bahá'í Social and Economic Development,* pp. 43–49.

Chapter 16

1. The Universal House of Justice, in *Lights of Guidance,* no. 1144.
2. The Universal House of Justice, *Messages from the Universal House of Justice,* no. 375.5
3. On behalf of Shoghi Effendi, quoted in ibid., no. 195.3a.
4. The Universal House of Justice, ibid., no. 19.5.

Bibliography

Works of Bahá'u'lláh

Epistle to the Son of the Wolf. 1st pocket-size ed. Translated by Shoghi Effendi. Wilmette, IL: Bahá'í Publishing Trust, 1988.

Gleanings from the Writings of Bahá'u'lláh. 1st pocket-size ed. Translated by Shoghi Effendi. Wilmette, IL: Bahá'í Publishing Trust, 1983.

The Hidden Words. Translated by Shoghi Effendi. Wilmette, IL: Bahá'í Publishing, 2002.

The Kitáb-i-Aqdas: The Most Holy Book. 1st pocket-size ed. Wilmette, IL: Bahá'í Publishing Trust, 1993.

The Kitáb-i-Íqán: The Book of Certitude. Translated by Shoghi Effendi. Wilmette, IL: Bahá'í Publishing, 2003.

Seven Valleys and the Four Valleys. New ed. Translated by Ali-Kuli Khan and Marzieh Gail. Wilmette, IL: Bahá'í Publishing Trust, 1991.

Tablets of Bahá'u'lláh Revealed after the Kitáb-i-Aqdas. Compiled by the Research Department of the Universal House of Justice. Translated by Habib Taherzadeh et al. Wilmette, IL: 1988.

Works of the Báb

Selections from the Writings of the Báb. Compiled by the Research Department of the Universal House of Justice. Translated by Habib Taherzadeh et al. Haifa: Bahá'í World Centre, 2006.

Works of 'Abdu'l-Bahá

'Abdu'l-Bahá in London: Addresses and Notes of Conversations. London: Bahá'í Publishing Trust, 1982.

Paris Talks: Addresses Given By 'Abdu'l-Bahá in Paris in 1911. 12th ed. London: Bahá'í Publishing Trust, 1995.

Promulgation of Universal Peace: Talks Delivered by 'Abdu'l-Bahá during His Visit to the United States and Canada in 1912. Compiled by Howard MacNutt. 2nd ed. Wilmette, IL: Bahá'í Publishing Trust, 1982.

Selections from the Writings of 'Abdu'l-Bahá. Compiled by the Research Department of the Universal House of Justice. Translated by a Committee at the Bahá'í World Center and Marzieh Gail. 1st pocket-size ed. Wilmette, IL: Bahá'í Publishing Trust, 1996.

Some Answered Questions. Compiled and translated by Laura Clifford Barney. 1st pocket-size ed. Wilmette, IL: Bahá'í Publishing Trust, 1984.

The Secret of Divine Civilization. Translated by Marzieh Gail with Ali-Kuli Khan. 1st pocket-sized ed. Wilmette, IL: Bahá'í Publishing Trust, 1990.

Tablets of the Divine Plan. 1st pocket-sized ed. Wilmette, IL: Bahá'í Publishing Trust, 1993.

Will and Testament of 'Abdu'l-Bahá. Wilmette, IL: Bahá'í Publishing Trust, 1944.

Works of Shoghi Effendi

Advent of Divine Justice. 1st pocket-size ed. Wilmette, IL: Bahá'í Publishing Trust, 1990.

Bahá'í Administration: Selected Messages 1922–1932. 7th ed. Wilmette, IL: Bahá'í Publishing Trust, 1974.

Citadel of Faith: Messages to America, 1947–1957. Wilmette, IL: Bahá'í Publishing Trust, 1965.

Directives from the Guardian. Compiled by Gertrude Garrida. New Delhi, Bahá'í Publishing Trust, 1973.

God Passes By. New ed. Wilmette, IL: Bahá'í Publishing Trust, 1974.

The World Order of Bahá'u'lláh: Selected Letters. 1st pocket-size ed. Wilmette, IL: Bahá'í Publishing Trust, 1991.

Compilations of Bahá'í Writings

Bahá'u'lláh, the Báb, and 'Abdu'l-Bahá. *Bahá'í Prayers: A Selection of Prayers Revealed by Bahá'u'lláh, the Báb, and 'Abdu'l-Bahá.* New ed. Wilmette, IL: Bahá'í Publishing Trust, 2003.

Bahá'u'lláh, the Báb, 'Abdu'l-Bahá, Shoghi Effendi, and the Universal House of Justice. *Compilation of Compilations,* vol. 1. Australia: Bahá'í Publications Australia, 1991.

Helen Hornby. Compiler. *Lights of Guidance.* New ed. New Delhi, India: Bahá'í Publishing Trust, 1994.

Other Works

Bahá'í International Community. *The Bahá'í World 2005–2006.* Haifa: World Centre Publications, 2007.

———. *The Bahá'í World 2002–2003.* Haifa: World Centre Publications, 2004.

———. *For the Betterment of the World.* Haifa: World Centre Publications, 2003.

———. *The Prosperity of Humankind.* Wilmette, IL: Bahá'í Publishing Trust, 1995.

Bahá'í World Center. *Century of Light.* Haifa: World Centre Publications, 2001.

Nabíl-i-A'zam [Muḥammad-i-Zarandí]. *The Dawn-Breakers: Nabíl's Narrative of the Days of the Bahá'í Revelation.* Translated and edited by Shoghi Effendi. Wilmette, IL: Bahá'í Publishing Trust, 1932.

National Spiritual Assembly of the Bahá'ís of the United States. *The Vision of Race Unity.* Wilmette, IL: Bahá'í Publishing Trust, 1991.

———. *Two Wings of a Bird,* Wilmette, IL: Bahá'í Publishing Trust, 1997.

Sours, Michael. *The Prophecies of Jesus.* Oxford: Oneworld Publications, 1991.

Universal House of Justice. *Individual Rights and Freedoms in the World Order of Bahá'u'lláh.* Wilmette, IL: Bahá'í Publishing Trust, 1988.

———. *Issues Related to the Study of the Bahá'í Faith.* Wilmette, IL: Bahá'í Publishing Trust, 1999.

———. *Messages from the Universal House of Justice. 1963–1986.* Wilmette, IL: Bahá'í Publishing Trust, 1996.

———. *Readings on Bahá'í Social and Economic Development.* West Palm Beach, FL: Palabra Publications, 2000.

Index

on peace and unity, 47
on perfecting behavior, 77
on power of unity, 66
on prayer, 75
on prejudice, 105–6
on progressive revelation,
    30–31
on pursuit of knowledge,
    78–79
sacrifice of, 157
on search for truth, 40
on slander and backbiting,
    119–20
on spiritual revolution,
    64–65
on state sovereignty, 49
on transformation of
    mankind, 62–63
on virtues, 22
on wealth, 152
on work as worship,
    149–50
writings of, 25, 66n,
    71–72, 76–77
Bayán, The, 167
beauty
    Christ and, 123–24
    as essential, 150–51
behavior
    of Bahá'í youth, 161
    of Bahá'ís, 57, 126
    to eliminate prejudice,
        107–9
    peace and patterns of, 52
    perfecting individual, 56,
        59, 61–62, 62–63, 77
    standards of, 207–8

as step to spirituality,
    4, 207
steps to changing vices
    and, 122–26
bird (analogy), 57, 116–17
birth (analogy), 46, 146
"Book, The"
    as proof of Manifestation,
        42–43
born-again Christians, 64
branches, 13
Buddha, 38
Bushrui, Suheil, 61n

C

calendar (Bahá'í), 88
Center for the Study of the
    Sacred Texts, 96
Center of the Covenant. *See*
    'Abdu'l-Bahá ('Abbás
    Effendi)
Central Organization for a
    Durable Peace, 51
certitude (religious). *See also*
    truth
    search for, 71–83, 75
charity, 153
childhood development
    (metaphor), 46–47
children
    development projects and,
        181
    education and, 82
    prejudice and, 107
    Ruhi Institute process and,
        202

developed world
  projects in, 179–81
development projects, 174,
  175–78
discrimination
  racial, 113
diversity
  of Bahá'í community, 109
  unity and, 57–58
Divine Messengers, 8

E

education
  Bahá'í schools and, 173
  of Bahá'í youth, 161, 163
  imperative of, 81–83
  in Iran, 173
  material *vs.* spiritual,
    167–68
  of the poor, 155
  prejudice and, 107
  responsibility for, 82, 83, 90
  Ruhi Institute process and,
    200–1, 202
educator
  high station of, 166–68
elections and electoral process
  delegates in, 95
  electors in, 92
  of Local Spiritual Assembly,
    91–94
  minority groups in, 111
  spiritual nature of, 92–93,
    97, 136
end times, 7
  Shoghi Effendi on, 48

English (language), 34
equality
  of men and women, 95–96,
    116–18
evils
  in United States, 188–89
Ewing, Sovaida, 61n
"eye of oneness"
  as gift from God, 69
  as metaphor, 65–68

F

faith
  tests of, 205–6
Farsi, 39n
fasting, 60n
fault-finding, 119, 120–21,
  123–24
Feast Days, 88
Festival of Riḍván, 11, 91
Five Year Plan, 198, 202
For the Betterment of the
  World, 175
forgiveness
  'Abdu'l-Bahá on, 125
  by African Americans, 114
  Bahá'u'lláh on, 102
  Christ's teachings on, 101
Four Year Plan, 197–98,
  199
freedom, personal, 57–58,
  135, 192–94
fund, Bahá'í, 155
future
  Bahá'í vision of, 45–58,
    183–87

Manifestation(s) of God. *See also* Prophet(s)
Báb, the, as, 15–16
Bahá'u'lláh as, 15–16
as catalysts, 36
characteristics of, 26
following Bahá'u'lláh, 38
gender of, 39
importance of, 26
missions of, 28, 29n
nature of, 25–29
as one divine being, 32n
progressive revelation and, 31
proofs of divine origin of, 147
as Prophets, 26
redemptive spiritual energy of, 33
renewing the world and, 37, 103
as revealing new religions, 36n
revelations of, 25n, 64
spiritual changes and, 35
spiritually dormant people and, 188
teachings of, 68, 75–77, 101
three proofs of, 42–44
materialism
in United States, 189–92
maturity (spiritual)
capacity for, 68–69
of individuals, 55, 59–60, 63, 85
meaning of, 66
practices to develop, 69

men
equality of women and, 95–96, 116–18
role in Universal House of Justice, 95–96
metaphors. *See* analogies and metaphors
Millennium. *See* end times
minority groups
electoral process and, 111
mirror (metaphor), 27–28, 69
Mírzá Ḥusayn-'Alí Núrí. *See* Bahá'u'lláh (Mírzá Ḥusayn-'Alí Núrí)
Mírzá Mihdí, 157
missions
of Bahá'u'lláh, 68–69
of Manifestations, 28, 29n
of religions, 1, 191
moonlight (analogy), 29
moral standards and teachings
of Bahá'ís, 61–62
renewal of, 68–69
Moses
as Manifestation of God, 8, 32n, 38
rejection of, 41
teachings of, 66n, 75
Most Great Peace, 47, 186
Mount Carmel, 96, 96n
Muḥammad. *See also* Islam
as Manifestation of God, 32n, 38
rejection of, 41
as "seal of the prophets," 31
teachings of, 66n, 75
Mullá Ḥusayn, 10n

*Turning Point for All Nations,
A,* 143
Twelfth Imam, 7–8
Two Wings of a Bird, 117
twofold process
of attaining peace, 50–53

U

United Nations, 51, 143,
144–45, 185–86
United States
Bahá'í Faith and, 183–94
racial prejudice in, 109–16
social justice in, 115–16
society of, 112
unity. *See also* oneness of
humanity
in consultation, 132–34
"eye of oneness" and,
65–68
Feast Days and, 88
justice and, 56
meaning of, 53–58
personal freedom and,
57–58
requirements for, 54–55
Shoghi Effendi on, 48–49
vices as barriers to, 119,
120–21
as work of Bahá'í Faith,
50, 53, 142
Universal House of Justice
'Abdu'l-Bahá on, 136–37
in Bahá'í administrative
order, 17, 87
development and, 171–72

on efforts of youth,
165–66
on electors and Assem-
blies, 92–93
establishment of, 197,
199
Ḥuqúqu'lláh and, 156
on justice and unity,
56–57
letters of, 76–77
operation of, 95–97
peace and, 51–52
on prejudice, 103–4
role of men in, 95–96
on service, 148–49,
162–64
on steps to spirituality,
206–7
on unity, 54–55

V

"Valley of Search, The," 72
vices
as barriers to unity, 119,
120–21
violence, 11
virtues, 22, 154
Virtues Project, 179–80
vision of the future
Bahá'í, 45–58
Vision of Race Unity, The, 115

W

war, 80–81
wealth, 151–54, 155

Baháʾí
PUBLISHING
and the Baháʾí Faith

Baháʾí Publishing produces books based on the teachings of the Baháʾí Faith. Founded more than 160 years ago, the Baháʾí Faith has spread to some 235 nations and territories and is now accepted by more than five and a half million people. The word "Baháʾí" means "follower of Baháʾuʾlláh." Baháʾuʾlláh, the founder of the Baháʾí Faith, asserted that he is the Messenger of God for all of humanity in this day. The cornerstone of his teachings is the establishment of the spiritual unity of humankind, which will be achieved by personal transformation and the application of clearly identified spiritual principles. Baháʾís also believe that there is but one religion and that all the Messengers of God—among them Abraham, Zoroaster, Moses, Krishna, Buddha, Jesus, and Muḥammad—have progressively revealed its nature. Together, the world's great religions are expressions of a single, unfolding divine plan. Human beings, not God's Messengers, are the source of religious divisions, prejudices, and hatreds.

The Baháʾí Faith is not a sect or denomination of another religion, nor is it a cult or a social movement. Rather, it is a globally recognized independent world religion founded on new books of scripture revealed by Baháʾuʾlláh.

Baháʾí Publishing is an imprint of the National Spiritual Assembly of the Baháʾís of the United States.

For more information about the Baháʾí Faith,
or to contact the Baháʾís near you, visit
http://www.bahai.us/
or call
1-800-22-UNITE

Other Books Available from Bahá'í Publishing

The Ascent of Society
THE SOCIAL IMPERATIVE IN PERSONAL SALVATION
John S. Hatcher
$19.95 U.S. / $22.95 CAN
Trade Paper
978-1-931847-52-0

An illuminating examination of the relationship between individual spiritual development and the collective advancement of civilization.

In *The Purpose of Physical Reality* Dr. John S. Hatcher compared the physical world to a classroom designed by God to stimulate individual spiritual growth and to prepare us for birth into a spiritual existence. But how does personal spiritual development translate into social experience? Is there a social imperative connected with individual spiritual growth? Is involvement with others necessary for one to evolve spiritually? Hatcher analyzes these questions and more in *The Ascent of Society: The Social Imperative in Personal Salvation*. This penetrating study describes the objective of personal spiritual growth as an "ever-expanding sense of self" that requires social relationships in order to develop. Hatcher focuses on the Bahá'í belief that human history is a divinely guided process in which spiritual principles are gradually and progressively expressed in social institutions. He demonstrates that the aspirant to spiritual transformation cannot view personal health and development as being possible apart from the progress of human society as a whole.

John S. Hatcher holds a BA and MA in English literature from Vanderbilt University and a PhD in English literature from the University of Georgia. He is the director of graduate studies in English literature at the University of South Florida, Tampa. A widely published poet and distinguished lecturer, he has written numerous books on literature, philosophy, and Bahá'í theology and scripture, including *Close Connections: The Bridge between Physical and Spiritual Reality, From the Auroral Darkness: The Life and Poetry of Robert E. Hayden, A Sense of History: The Poetry of John Hatcher, The Ocean of His Words: A Reader's Guide to the Art of Bahá'u'lláh,* and *The Purpose of Physical Reality.* He and his family live on a farm near Plant City, Florida.

Hidden Gifts
FINDING BLESSINGS IN THE STRUGGLES OF LIFE
Brian Kurzius
$10.95 U.S. / $13.95 CAN
Trade Paper
978-1-931847-48-3

Have you ever wondered why we have problems and tests in our lives? Where do they come from? What is the most effective way to handle them? We may not see it, but there just might be a multitude of gifts hidden among our problems and tests.

In *Hidden Gifts: Finding Blessings in the Struggles of Life*, author Brian Kurzius searches the Bahá'í scriptures for answers to the meaning of human suffering. What is the value of suffering in our lives? How do we decide on the best course of action? Are there qualities and attributes we can develop to help us more effectively face life's challenges? The answers to these questions and others are found in this spiritually edifying collection of extracts from Bahá'í scripture.

Over the course of many years, author Brian Kurzius has studied the subject of human suffering extensively. His research increasingly drew him to the writings of the Bahá'í Faith on the subject. He now offers workshops and lectures frequently about finding gifts in the struggles of life. Kurzius is also the author of *Fire & Gold: Benefiting from Life's Test*. Brian and his wife, Christine, live in Haifa, Israel, where they work for the Bahá'í World Center.

The Secret of Divine Civilization
'Abdu'l-Bahá
$9.95 U.S. / $12.95 CAN
978-1-931847-51-3

An outstanding treatise on the social and spiritual progress both of nations and of individuals.

The Secret of Divine Civilization is a thorough explanation of the view of the Bahá'í Faith on the true nature of civilization. It contains an appealing and universal message inspiring world-mindedness and soliciting the highest human motives and attributes for the establishment of a spiritual society. Written by 'Abdu'l-Bahá in the late nineteenth century as a letter to the rulers and people of Persia, it is still profoundly relevant today as a guide to creating a peaceful and productive world.

ʿAbdu'l-Bahá, meaning in Arabic "Servant of the Glory," was the title assumed by ʿAbbás Effendi (1844–1921), the eldest son and appointed successor of Bahá'u'lláh, the Prophet and Founder of the Bahá'í Faith. A prisoner since the age of nine, ʿAbdu'l-Bahá shared a lifetime of imprisonment and exile with his father at the hands of the Ottoman Empire. He spent his entire life in tireless service to, and promotion of, Bahá'u'lláh's teachings.

A Way Out of the Trap
A TEN-STEP PROGRAM FOR SPIRITUAL GROWTH
Nathan Rutstein
$10.95 U.S. / $13.95 CAN
Trade Paper
978-1-931847-40-7

An easy-to-follow guide for people of all faiths to reconnect with God and live more fulfilling lives.

A Way Out of the Trap: A Ten-Step Program for Spiritual Growth offers a process by which the spiritually hungry can find the faith, hope, and spiritual sustenance needed to break out of the trap of hopelessness. Author Nathan Rutstein outlines a spiritual path that can help people of all faiths to reconnect with God. The result is a practical guide to understanding the purpose of life and how to live it.

Author, lecturer, college educator, and former network journalist, Nathan Rutstein has written numerous books about life, spirituality, racism, education, and the oneness of humanity. He is also one of the founders of the Institute for the Healing of Racism in the United States, lecturing at scores of colleges, universities, and government institutions on the subject.

To view our complete catalog,
please visit http://Books.Bahai.us

Printed in the United States
200064BV00004B/118-276/A

9 781931 847445